Geography Mysteries

Warm Up
with Garfield

Created by
JIM DAVIS

Written by
Marjorie Frank

Incentive Publications, Inc.
Nashville, TN

To Parents and Teachers

- Use each geography mystery as a short warm-up to stimulate social studies exploration and reasoning, and to build excitement about geography, OR use any one as the basis for a longer geography lesson focused on the related topic, concept, or process.

- Use the mysteries to complement ANY social studies course. The geographic knowledge, research skills, and thinking processes involved in these mysteries are used in ALL fields of social studies.

- Use the mysteries randomly, or choose one that specifically fits a standard, skill, or process.

- Student "detectives" will need geography tools for most of the mysteries. Have plenty of world maps, globes, atlases, and other map resources available. It will be helpful for students to have access to an up-to-date world almanac and the Internet or a good encyclopedia. Use the Internet sparingly. Students should strengthen skills by searching maps rather than finding quick answers on the Internet.

- ALWAYS take time for students to ponder strategies used in solving the mystery. Encourage them to discuss the steps they took and explain the reasons for their solution. Ask students to share new things they learned while solving the mystery.

- Help students connect the concepts and processes of each mystery to their real lives.

- Discuss the connection between the Garfield cartoon and the geography mystery.

Notes:

- The table on page 93 lists geography topics, concepts, and processes sharpened by the mysteries. This will help you find an activity connected to a specific standard, concept, or skill.

- Make copies of the World Time Zone Map on page 94 available for solving mysteries involving time zones.

Illustrations by Paws, Inc.
Additional Artwork by Kathleen Bullock
Cover by Kathleen Bullock and Kris Sexton
Edited by Jill Norris

ISBN 978-0-86530-750-6

1   2   3   4   5   6   7   8   9   10   12   11   10   09

PRINTED IN THE UNITED STATES OF AMERICA
www.incentivepublications.com

A CAT'S INNATE CURIOSITY CAUSES HIM TO EXPLORE THE WORLD

What do you get when you send a curious, witty cat around the world to solve a host of tangled geography mysteries? You get dozens of dilemmas that need application of social studies concepts and skills, plus—you are drawn into a whole lot of adventuresome fun.

GARFIELD

Garfield is a clever cat who gets into all sorts of quandaries—at home and all over the world. He easily turns into "Garfield the Explorer," seeking out solutions to conundrums and mysteries.

In any setting, Garfield is good at using the questioning and problem-solving skills that are basic to finding landforms, locations, and important geographical sites (especially when there is food to find). And he never stays lost for long! He can find his way home from anywhere.

&

GEOGRAPHY MYSTERIES

are short, intriguing tasks that challenge you to find something, solve a crime, or untangle a problem. To sort these out, you will need to apply your understanding of world geography and use your best social studies analysis and research skills. But you won't be alone! Garfield will come along to be your investigative companion—adding his humorous comments, questions, and insights to every mystery.

Garfield has a sharp, curious mind and likes to draw conclusions about people, places, and situations in the world around him. So naturally, it makes sense to combine his adventures with social studies investigations! The result of this mixture is a collection of 88 intriguing, brain-stretching mysteries that are just the right length to warm you up to geography.

Contents

⁛ About the Geography Mysteries

AHH,
TRAVEL
BROCHURES

- Each activity starts with a curious story that sets the stage for the mystery. This introduction includes some details or clues related to the situation. Then the Mystery is stated in the form of a question. To solve the mystery, you will need to apply geography skills, concepts, and information. In addition, you will need to make inferences, analyze and compare information, and draw reasonable conclusions.

- There are many kinds of mysteries in this collection. All of them will challenge you to use the skills and processes that you need for your geography class as well as your daily life.

- You will find that the Mysteries make use of many different geography concepts and topics, such as:

physical-cultural regions	map use	world nations
human-made features	directions	continents
resources and products	weather	hemispheres
neighbors and borders	climate	major cities
latitude and longitude	landforms	natural processes
human-land interactions	water bodies	Earth changes
map scale and distances	ocean features	traditions
locations (find and compare)	governments	time zones
geography-history connections	land bodies	economics

⁛ How to Use This Book

- Read each Mystery all the way through. Notice what supplies you will need (maps, globes, almanac, measuring tools, etc.). Gather these before you start.

- You can tackle a Mystery alone, but sometimes it is fun to work with a partner or small group. If you are having trouble with a Mystery, get someone to join you in pondering the question or doing the research.

- With each Mystery, try to identify the geography concepts and processes that you are using as you find a solution.

- When you reach a solution, explain how you found it. Compare your solution and strategies with someone else's.

- When you finish each one, make note of something new you learned about geography while you figured out the answer to the mystery question.

- All of these Mysteries will stretch your brain. Have fun trying them out. And, have fun with Garfield!

The Long-Distance Pizza

As curious a cat as Garfield is, his strongest instincts are to stay right at home (preferably sleeping or eating). Garfield is happy, though, when Jon returns from his world travels with a pizza. Jon brings this slightly stale pizza from the capital of a nation miles away.

Follow the clues to solve the mystery.

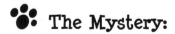 Clues:

- The capital city is on a coastline.

- The city is farther south than another national capital, Bogota.

- The city is farther north than Pretoria.

- It lies in two hemispheres different from those where Ottawa is located.

- It is farther west than Wellington.

- It is farther east than Tokyo.

- This capital's nation shares an island and land with another nation.

The Mystery:

From which world capital did Jon bring the pizza?

Name:_____

Geography Mysteries—Warm Up with Garfield

Follow the Lasagna

The lure of good lasagna is strong enough to overcome Garfield's resistance to leaving his cozy bed or reliable refrigerator. So he heads off to big cities around the world searching for more of his favorite dish.

May 1

Garfield follows his nose to a little cafe located at about **35°S, 58°W.**

Where is Garfield?

The latitude and longitude descriptions give precise locations of the places Garfield visits. Identify each city where he tastes lasagna. (Of course, he does far more than just taste!)

May 5

Ocean breezes bring the scent of lasagna to tickle Garfield's nose at this location: **34°S, 151°E.**

Where is Garfield?

The Mystery:

Where is Garfield on each of these days?

May 8

The noisy streets of this city at about **6°S, 106°E** do not distract Garfield from his quest.

Where is Garfield?

May 14

On his way to eat lasagna at about **18°N, 77°W,** Garfield stops to shake his belly to reggae music.

Where is Garfield?

May 18

He may hear over 200 different languages spoken in this capital city located at about **4°S, 15°E.** It's a good thing Garfield understands "food" in any language.

Where is Garfield?

May 22

The lasagna is so rich, creamy, and plentiful that Garfield cannot move after eating this batch. So he just stays here for a long, long time— at a location of about **41°N, 14°E.**

Where is Garfield?

Name:_____

The Fraudulent Paintings

While Garfield is in Paris, a fraud is discovered at the Louvre Museum. A priceless painting, *l'audace de chat*, has been replaced by a copy. Versions of this painting are hidden at several Parisian landmarks. An anonymous call tips police to the locations and the clue that one of these is the masterpiece.

L'AUDACE DE CHAT—THE DARING CAT. THAT MUST BE A PAINTING OF ME!

- Garfield tags along with police as they pick up paintings at these sites featured on the map:
  - a) directly east of Musée du Louvre
  - b) northwest of Parc des Buttes-Chaumont
  - c) on island in Seine River
  - d) directly southeast of La Sorbonne
  - e) farthest west on Les Champs Elysées
  - f) just north of Boulevard Périphérique

- Of the paintings retrieved, the one hidden farthest from Parc Citroën is the original.

🐾 The Mystery:

At which famous site in Paris is the real painting hidden?

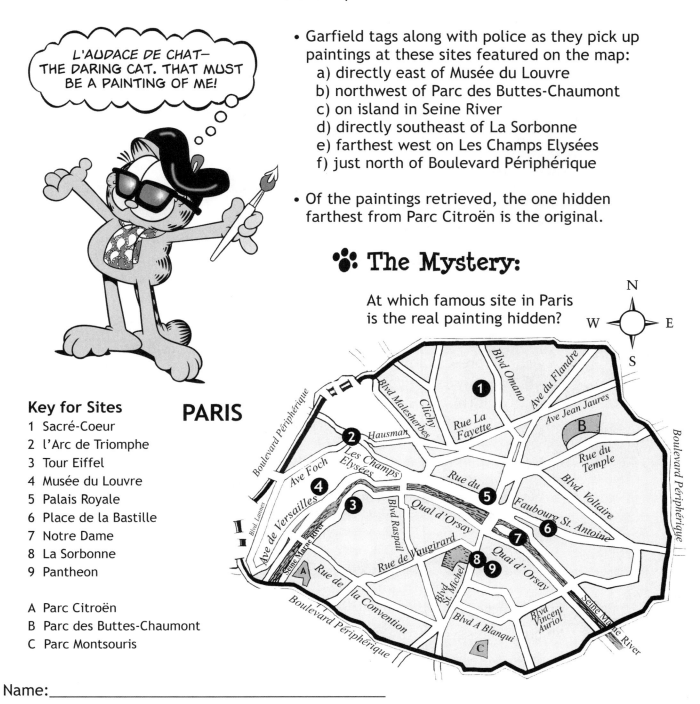

Key for Sites
1 Sacré-Coeur
2 l'Arc de Triomphe
3 Tour Eiffel
4 Musée du Louvre
5 Palais Royale
6 Place de la Bastille
7 Notre Dame
8 La Sorbonne
9 Pantheon

A Parc Citroën
B Parc des Buttes-Chaumont
C Parc Montsouris

Name:_____

The Hidden Artifacts

Taking a break from those luscious English scones and cream, Garfield goes undercover in London as a palace guard. Word has it that a valuable artifact given as a gift to the queen has been smuggled out of the palace and is now hidden in one of those tall hats. Garfield may look sleepy, but his sharp eyes watch for suspicious behavior.

This smuggled artifact is one of the following:

- bronze statue of a Mesopotamian goddess
- piece of obsidian pottery from Sardinia
- Samurai dagger
- pre-Columbian Aztec mask
- tiny Tang Dynasty vase
- Greek terra-cotta figurine
- scrap of a priceless Persian tapestry

The missing artifact originally came from a place near a large peninsula, a sea, a large gulf, a mountain range, and countries such as present-day Iraq, Iran, and Syria.

The Mystery:

Which of the seven artifacts could be hidden under a guard's hat?

Name:_____

8

Vacation by the Sea

One member of Garfield's family is excited about the island vacation. But where, actually, is this place? All Garfield knows is that it's in some sea. He's wary about this trip and is just hoping that the fish are plentiful.

Jon and Garfield take a train to Chicago, then fly east to New York City. From there, they fly directly east for 11 hours. After doing a little island hopping, they end up at a resort on a sea that is just about the same latitude as New York City. The sea is bordered by six countries, with a strait that opens on the south end to another, smaller sea.

⁂ The Mystery:

What sea can they see from their beachfront resort?

Name:_____

Geography Mysteries—Warm Up with Garfield

Race Against Time

HONG KONG SOMALIA BRAZIL

THE FLYING ACE COMES TO THE RESCUE!

At 5:00 PM on Tuesday, Garfield was sampling sushi in Hong Kong. Meanwhile in Somalia, a rare, poisonous insect stung a fellow cat. Garfield was called upon to help. His challenge was to pick up a sample of blood from the victim, take it to a lab in Brazil where an antidote would be made, and get it back to Somalia. In order to survive, the cat needed the antidote within 48 hours of the sting.

- Garfield got the news and hurried to the airport. He was able to leave Hong Kong at 7:00 PM Hong Kong time—two hours after the incident.

- The flight from Hong Kong to Mogadishu, Somalia, took seven hours.

- It took four hours to get to the site of the incident, get back to the airport, and be ready to take off.

- The flight to Manaus, Brazil, was fourteen hours long.

- Garfield waited in Manaus for the antidote to be made and delivered to him. He was able to leave the ground just two hours after the time he arrived.

- The flight back to Somalia took thirteen hours. After he arrived, another two hours passed before Garfield could reach the victim.

 ## The Mystery:

When did Garfield reach the victim with the antidote?

Did this happen in time to save the victim?

Name:_____

The Burrito Burglary

YOU CHASE THE BANDIT WHILE I STAY HERE AND PROTECT THE REST OF THE BURRITOS

CHOMP

GULP

SWALLOW

YUM

Garfield stumbled upon the burrito of his dreams at a little shack in Puerto San Jose, Guatemala. Just as he was standing outside relishing in the ecstasy of his discovery, a burrito bandit was slinking out the back door with a pocketful of burritos and the secret recipe.

Local law enforcement officers chased the burrito bandit to a string of cities throughout Central and South America.

They tracked him from **TEGUCIGALPA**
TO LEÓN
  TO CASTRIES
   TO VALENCIA
    TO RECIFE
     TO OAXACA
      TO SÃO PAULO
       TO CARACAS
        TO MANAGUA
         TO SAN SALVADOR
          TO PORT-AU-PRINCE
           TO PORTO ALEGRE
            TO MONTEGO BAY,
where they caught the culprit trying to sell the recipe.

🐾 The Mystery:

How many different countries did the officers visit during their search?

Name:_____

Suspicious Cargo

FRAGILE CREAM PUFFS?

LIVE PIRANHAS?

HMMM... GOLD BRICKS?

STOLEN PEPPERONI?

A RARE RHINO?

A MILLION MEATBALLS?

What's the cargo in Garfield's truck? Even he doesn't know. He has been told that this load cannot be put on an airplane, and that he will be well paid to get it to the destination safely. Also, he has been asked to drive carefully, avoiding sudden stops and bumpy roads.

Although the mysterious cargo piques his curiosity, he is satisfied with the large supply of pizza, doughnuts, and sardines he's been given. And he hopes to find even more food in this interesting part of the world.

The truck is loaded in Saskatoon, Saskatchewan, Canada. The final destination is Charlottetown, Prince Edward Island, Canada.

🐾 The Mysteries:

Can the trip actually be made by truck (on land or bridges, with no need for ferries or other boats)?

What do you suspect is in the truck?

What leads you to this suspicion?

Name:_____

The Abducted Scientist

Geologist Dr. Carlotta Gold has been abducted. Her secret research led to the location of a gold vein—one of the largest ever discovered. But the word got out. She has been captured and taken somewhere deep into Africa. Garfield and friends just happen to be in the area. The curious cat, his owner, and their dog, are on their way to explore the capital city of Khartoum. When a tip comes in about Dr. Gold's location, their plane is diverted for a rescue attempt.

Garfield's plane has just taken off from the capital city of Dakar. It is headed due east along the same line of latitude as Dakar.

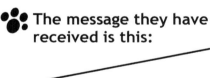 **The message they have received is this:**

Dr. Gold's location:

Stay on the same course until you are directly south of Khartoum. She has been sighted on the banks of the last major river you will cross before turning north to Khartoum.

Proceed with caution. Her captors are unsavory characters.

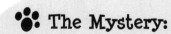 **The Mystery:**

What is the river that the rescuers need to find?

Name: _____

Caught on Camera

The camera is always clicking when Garfield travels. (Usually, he wants to be IN the picture.) Right now, he is traveling in Asia with his owner, Jon. All the pictures in his camera are from this area of the world.

The Mystery:

Which of these pictures could be in his camera?

1. Garfield diving into the deepest, coldest lake in the world

2. Jon riding an elephant in a country where the elephant is a national symbol

3. Garfield with a turtle in the Galapagos Islands

4. a boatload of tourists looking for the Loch Ness Monster

5. Garfield meeting a Siberian tiger

6. a shot looking up at the world's highest waterfall

7. scenes from six different countries that end with the letters "stan"

8. Garfield wrestling a crocodile on the banks of the world's longest river

9. Jon paddling a canoe in a fjord

10. Garfield making friends with a Bengali tiger

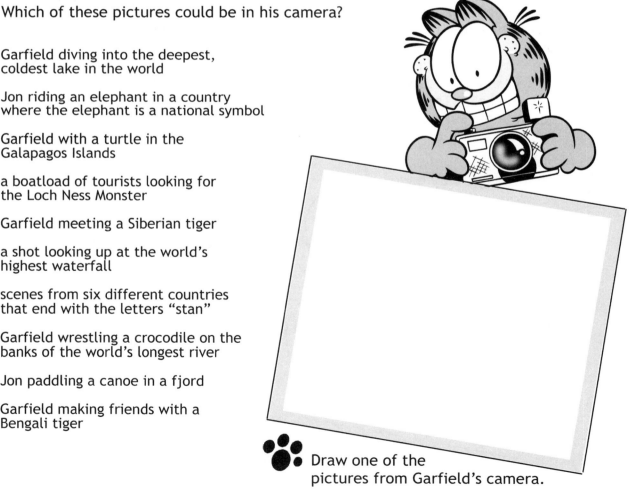

Draw one of the pictures from Garfield's camera.

Name:_____

Jungle Secrets

Jungles hold secrets. The deep, thick rainforests are natural places for someone to stash stolen diamonds, hide a runaway robber, or bury bags of silver. You might find rebel hideouts, exiled dictators, people escaping from angry relatives or creditors, partners plotting devious deeds, or just folks who have private dealings they don't want to share.

Garfield is off to a few of the world's jungles to snoop into some such secrets. It is uncanny how cats can wiggle their way into the most clandestine situations.

His travels take him to each of the countries listed below. Not all the stops are in jungles. Sometimes the lure of exotic fish, spectacular enchiladas, steamy peanut stew, or fresh banana pudding call for a diversion from the trip plan.

The Mystery:

Which of the stops are in countries that are NOT home to a jungle?

Stop # 1:	Belize		Stop # 11:	Thailand
Stop # 2:	Venezuela		Stop # 12:	Brazil
Stop # 3:	Congo		Stop # 13:	India
Stop # 4:	Burma		Stop # 14:	Madagascar
Stop # 5:	South Africa		Stop # 15:	Australia
Stop # 6:	Argentina		Stop # 16:	Algeria
Stop # 7:	El Salvador		Stop # 17:	Peru
Stop # 8:	Costa Rica		Stop # 18:	Malaysia
Stop # 9:	Mexico		Stop # 19:	Greece
Stop # 10:	Honduras		Stop # 20:	Liberia

Name:_____

The Priceless Guitar

This guitar was said to be priceless. That's because the owner would not sell it for any price. But, alas, the owner fell on hard times, and put the guitar up for auction in a European city.

Garfield, that lucky cat and revered musician, got a chance to play the guitar for the prospective buyers who came to the auction.

There were 15 of them—each from one of the following European countries:

Austria, Belgium, Bulgaria, Finland, France, Greece, Hungary, Ireland, Kosovo, Lithuania, Monaco, Montenegro, Portugal, Sweden, and the United Kingdom.

The guitar sold for $2.3 million euros.

The Mysteries:

Which buyers would have to convert from their home currency in order to buy the guitar?

How much would that guitar cost (today) in American dollars?

How much would that guitar cost (today) in UK currency (the pound)?

Name:_____

A Curious Message

The usually lethargic Garfield, snoozing on a beach, sits up and takes notice when a bottle washes ashore. He wakes up even more when he reads the note in the bottle.

From the curious message, Garfield infers that the writer is someone stranded on an island somewhere in the world.

He starts listing islands he can remember from his travels:

Iceland	Greenland
Guam	Marshall Islands
U.S. Virgin Islands	Falkland Islands
Crete	Sardinia
Japanese Islands	Philippines
Borneo	Cuba
Madagascar	Jamaica
Pago Pago	Aleutian Islands
Fiji	Sri Lanka

Marooned kwajalein I think

The Mystery:

Which of the islands on Garfield's list is most likely to be near the location of the marooned writer?

Name:_____

Close to Home

Jon is planning a vacation trip by car. He won't tell Garfield the destination, and this is driving Garfield nuts. Jon will only say that they are visiting a major tourist attraction in their own country.

Garfield knows that Jon likes to drive no more than 1000 miles each way from their central Indiana home, so he starts looking up attractions and landmarks that might be within that distance. Then he shifts his energies to packing up a food supply for the many hours in the car.

Here's Garfield's list of some U.S. tourist attractions:

- Anasazi Indian Cliff Dwellings
- Rock and Roll Hall of Fame
- Everglades National Park
- Niagara Falls
- Carlsbad Caverns
- Gateway Arch
- The Alamo
- Mt. Rushmore
- Old Faithful Geyser
- Baseball Hall of Fame
- Mammoth Cave
- Death Valley

🐾 The Mystery:

How many of the locations on Garfield's list are NOT realistic possibilities for this trip?

Name:_____

Trekking to Treasure

Recently discovered maps of the Treasure Islands have an X marked at the highest point on each island. Does this mean there is treasure buried on every island? The treasure hunters want to find out. So they sail to each island, grab their shovels, and trek to the highest spot. After the search, they hike back down to the boat (with or without treasure).

THOSE TREASURE HUNTERS ARE IN FOR A SURPRISE — I BURIED SIX DOZEN FREEZE-DRIED PIZZAS AT EACH LOCATION!

AND A BOX OF CRACKERS FOR POLLY?

🐾 The Mystery:

How far (in vertical distance up and down) do the treasure hunters trek?

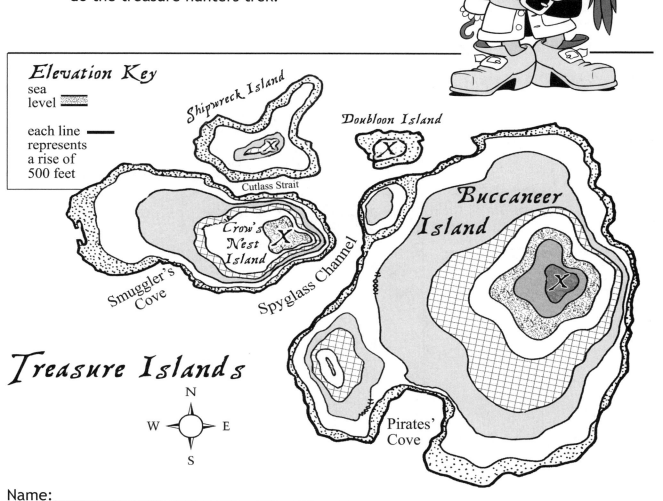

Elevation Key

sea level

each line ——— represents a rise of 500 feet

Shipwreck Island

Doubloon Island

Cutlass Strait

Crow's Nest Island

Buccaneer Island

Smuggler's Cove

Spyglass Channel

Pirates' Cove

Treasure Islands

N
W — E
S

Name:_____

The Unasked Question

In the final round of a geography bee, judges submitted questions about physical geographic features. Garfield got all the answers correct. When the bee was over and the prize had been awarded, it was discovered that one judge's question had not been asked. Garfield agreed to answer that last question—just to prove his geography expertise. His answer was right!

The Geography-Bee Questions

1. What is a fumarole?

2. Where is an alluvial deposit found?

3. What process is named by the word "orogeny"?

4. If you were lost in a savanna, where would you be?

5. What mixes with fog to form smog?

6. When you explore an erg, what is beneath your feet?

7. Where would you find the antipode to your current location?

8. If you're caught in a cataract, where are you?

9. What does a river meet at a confluence?

10. What carries loess?

11. ?????

🐾 **The Mystery:** What was the unasked question?

Name:_____

Stranded in the Strait

It's amazing how many straits connect bodies of water in this world! Garfield and Odie are determined to explore all of them. One strait seems to capture them—literally. The current keeps them from moving forward. An abandoned freighter blocks the exit behind them.

They are stranded!

HOW DO WE GET OUT OF THIS *STRAIT*JACKET?

🐾 The Mystery:

Where are Garfield and Odie?

- Strait of Gibraltar
- Straits of Mackinac
- Bass Strait
- Straits of Florida
- Strait of Sicily
- Cook Strait
- Strait of Malacca
- Hecate Strait
- Strait of Magellan
- La Perouse Strait
- Strait of Hormuz

After two days, their food is gone (a disaster for Garfield). They radio Jon for help, but their message is unclear. He only gets these scattered bits of information as to their whereabouts:

between an island and a peninsula

above 40°S latitude

separates two different countries

joins two oceans

south of 20°N latitude

REPEAT THAT, PLEASE

Name:_____

Geography Mysteries—Warm Up with Garfield

Emergency Delivery

A salmon cannery in Selawik, Alaska, is out of cans! The whole season's catch of fresh salmon is in danger of going to waste. It will take a hearty dog team to get to seven locations around the state to pick up cans and deliver them to the cannery before that fish is unusable.

Garfield takes off from Yukutat, Alaska, with a fresh team of dogs and one thing on his mind: the free salmon that is waiting for him at the end of the trip.

He stops in these towns (in this order) to pick up cans: Tok, Goodnews Bay, Holy Cross, Rampart, Chicken, Coldfoot, and Deadhorse. The last leg of the trip is from Deadhorse to Selawik.

🐾 The Mysteries:

Which of these sequences of directions is right for Garfield to follow on this trip?

1. NW, SW, NE, NE, SE, N, NE, S

2. NW, NW, E, NE, E, W, NE, SW

3. W, N, NE, NE, SE, NW, NE, SW

4. NW, SW, NE, NE, SE, NW, NE, S

5. NW, SW, NE, NE, SE, NW, NE, SW

Will Garfield cross the Yukon River on his trip?

Name:_____

22

The Missing Microchip

From his vacation spot in Mexico, Garfield hears the news: A microchip containing top secret codes has been stolen from NASA. It is thought that this will be sold to someone who intends to dangerously disrupt communications from dozens of satellites.

By some strange coincidence, the thieves have Garfield mixed up with the sinister buyer. Every day a bag of chips is delivered to his hotel room. A clue is written on one chip in the bag. When he puts all these clues together, Garfield will know where to pick up the microchip. But first, he must eat all the chips.

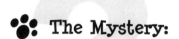

The Mystery:

Where is the missing microchip?

I'M GLAD THESE ARE MACRO-CHIPS!

#1 north of the equator

#2 capital city of a province

#3 11°30'E longitude

#5 once home to Leonardo da Vinci

#4 country that touches the Adriatic Sea

#6 building houses the "David" sculpture

#8 in a crack under the left little toe

#7 site of Ponte Vecchio over the Arno River

Name:_____

The Elusive Recipe

Garfield opted to stay home while Jon went on vacation in Hawaii. Each time Jon attended a luau, he knew Garfield had made a mistake to miss this trip. When he tasted the mouthwatering kalua pig served at a luau in Hilo, he decided he must get the recipe so he could cook some for Garfield back home.

No one seemed to have the recipe. Jon flew from island to island following tips, without success. The night before he was to fly home from Lihue, he got the best lead: The recipe could be found in the back of a small grocery store in Hana. Jon took a chance. Early in the morning, he rented a helicopter and flew in a straight line from Lihue to Hana.

 ## The Mystery:

Which of these land and water features did Jon cross on his trip to Hana?

a. Waianae Mountains

b. Koolau Mountains

c. Mauna Loa

d. Pearl Harbor

e. Kauai Channel

f. Kaiwi Channel

g. Pailolo Channel

h. Mamala Bay

i. Island of Molokai

j. Island of Maui

k. Island of Hawaii

l. Island of Kauai

m. Island of Lanai

n. Island of Oahu

o. Waimea Canyon

p. Wailuku River

Name:_____

24

The Space Stowaway

During a tour of some USA tourist attractions, Garfield slunk away from the crowd and found an out-of-the-way corner to take a nap. It turns out that the cozy space he found was a space capsule—and now he finds himself in space!

He did not intend to be a stowaway, but here he is, looking down at Earth. At this moment, he catches sight of all or part of the northern, eastern, and southern hemispheres.

OUT OF THIS WORLD!

The Mysteries:

Which of the views below is the one that Garfield sees? (Circle the number.)

What continent(s) does Garfield NOT see in this view?

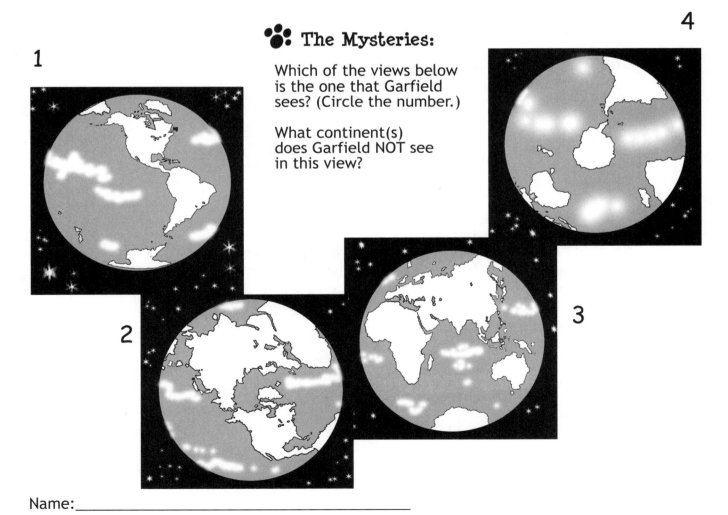

1

2

3

4

Name:_____

Vanished at the Peak

Things have been disappearing on mountain-climbing expeditions. Shortly after parties reach the peak, some vital supply seems to vanish into thin air.

- Oxygen tanks vanished on Mt. Kilimanjaro.
- Tents vanished on Mt. Wade.
- All the picks and axes vanished on Fujisan.
- Sleeping bags vanished on Pikes Peak.
- The food supply vanished on Mt. Cotopaxi.
- Cellphones vanished on Mt. Cook.
- Sunscreen vanished on Mont Blanc.

Garfield and Odie are currently in South America near one of the sites of a disappearance. They are invited to join the search for lost items. It's a lot of work to climb a mountain.

Garfield is considering this offer.

 **The Mystery:**

What vanished from the mountain close to Garfield's location?

Name:_____

The Coffee Caper

I'M FINE! IT'S ONLY MY TWELFTH CUP OF JAVA TODAY

A highly caffeinated crew of culprits concocted a clever coffee caper. They stole prizewinning gourmet coffee beans from the hills of Colombia and sold them for a very high price to a coffee dealer somewhere in Europe.

Garfield, coffee expert that he is, agrees to taste-test drinks in cafes throughout Europe. He is sure that he can identify that coffee when he drinks it.

Garfield drinks coffee in these cities: Tiranë, Riga, Dublin, Marseilles, Amsterdam, Manchester, Valencia, Zagreb, Sofia, Naples, Tartu, Odessa, and Lisbon.

Garfield identifies the smuggled coffee at a tiny cafe down a quiet side street in a city northeast of Istanbul. He gathers enough evidence to provide the police with grounds for a search. Indeed, they raid the adjoining coffee-roasting business and find the beans!

 The Mystery:

In what country does Garfield find the stolen beans?

I THINK GARFIELD IS FULL OF BEANS!

Name:_____

Suspects on the Slopes

While skiers enjoy the powdery slopes, six sneaky thieves rob the Summit Lodge. One packs the money and they all ski away. They are all dressed alike to confuse anyone who might try to catch up with the cash.

Unfortunately for the crooks, Garfield witnesses the robbery, noticing that the skier with the money is the one who just finished a tuna sandwich at the restaurant. Garfield only has to follow his nose as he heads out to the slopes.

Garfield follows the scent down Stomach Drop Hill, cuts under the lift to Broken Trail, skis to the intersection of Broken Trail and Big Bump Run, cuts straight over to Demon Run, above Half Way Hut to the junction of Loony Loop and Treacherous Trail. There the scent of tuna fish becomes overpowering as a skier runs right into Garfield.

🐾 The Mystery:

Which skier suspect has the cash? (Circle the suspect. Find all suspects by the X's.)

Name:_____

Cave Ciphers

When Garfield hears about the coded message rumored to be written on some cave walls, he gets into his cave attire and joins the search. That's because the message reveals the secret location of some buried treasure—a chest full of the rarest caviar.

Each of the first four caves he visits holds a coded word. The final three caves hold the cipher (clues to break the code). He writes the coded words in order, then uses the cipher to substitute letters. This gives him the location of the last cave—where the chest is buried.

WHAT DOES THE WELL-DRESSED CAVE EXPLORER WEAR?

CIPHERS FROM THE CAVE WALLS

PANDALIN CAVE, MYANMAR		ODGV
DRAGON'S LAIR, POLAND		MXSVE
EISRIESENWELT ICE CAVE, AUSTRIA		TC
MAMMOTH CAVE, KENTUCKY, USA		STDFRVE
SARAWAK CHAMBER, BORNEO	T = O, R = M, F = I, M = C	
LASCAUX CAVE, FRANCE	X = A, S = V, O = B, C = F	
CANGO CAVES, SOUTH AFRICA	V = E, D = L, G = U, E = S	

 **The Mystery:**

In what location (and in what country) will he find the caviar?

Name:_____

Geography Mysteries—Warm Up with Garfield

The Recovered Hockey Puck

Garfield goes undercover as a hockey pro to recover a precious black diamond. A scheming thief embedded the diamond in a hockey puck, then shipped dozens of pucks to hockey rinks and teams across Canada to throw authorities off the track of the diamond.

With his hockey skills, it is easy for Garfield to get invited to play games in all the places the diamond is suspected to be. (He must hit that puck in order to feel the presence of the diamond.) So he plays hockey in dozens of Canadian towns—from the border of Alaska, in the Rocky Mountains, along Hudson Bay, on the shores of Lake Superior, and all the way to Nova Scotia and Newfoundland.

One frigid night, Garfield plays at a rink on an island in a province bordering the Northwest Territories, Manitoba, and the Hudson Strait.

He hits a puck that has a different weight, and he knows he has found the one that holds the diamond.

🐾 The Mystery:

In what Canadian province did Garfield recover the hockey puck?

Name:_____

Arachnid Encounter

Garfield's travels take him to a place he has never been—a place that is home to the largest spider in the world.

Most visitors shudder at the tales of this arachnid. But Garfield, that fierce opponent of insects and spiders, is not daunted. Even though the goliath birdeater tarantula can grow to be one foot long, it is still no match for Garfield.

THE BIGGER THEY ARE, THE HARDER THEY FALL — NO MATTER WHERE THEY LIVE

The Mystery:

In what countries might Garfield be when he meets a goliath?

Name:_____

Separated on the Serengeti

Serengeti sounds a lot like "spaghetti," so Garfield is hoping to find some food out here. He's so focused on his stomach that he wanders away from the guide and the truck and loses track of where he is going. What's worse: He gets separated from his safari partner, Odie.

FORGET ODIE — WHAT ABOUT THE PROVISIONS?

The Mystery:

While Odie and Garfield are wandering the Serengeti looking for each other, which of these things are they NOT likely to encounter?

- ROAMING ZEBRAS
- THE LARGEST OVERLAND MIGRATION OF ANIMALS
- GAME RESERVES
- GRASSLANDS
- ROVING GRIZZLY BEARS
- THE MARA RIVER
- NATIONAL PARKS
- YEAR-ROUND RAINFALL
- A BORDER BETWEEN TWO COUNTRIES
- HERDS OF WILDEBEASTS
- ROAMING ANTELOPES

Name:_____

The Botched Train Robbery

When the Diesel brothers planned to rob a train, they got creative. They decided to lead a herd of cattle onto the train tracks, stop the train, heist the safe full of gold, and cart it away on super-charged trucks. In addition, they thought it would be cool to do this at the site of a famous train robbery from the past. So they chose one of these historic robberies:

- The Great Train Robbery (1963)
- The Bezdany Raid (1908)
- The Wilcox Train Robbery (1899)
- The Kakori Train Robbery (1925)
- The Great Gold Robbery of 1855

Their plan may have been inventive, but it was far from clever or careful. Somehow, one of the brothers (Doyle) ended up locked inside the safe while the cows stormed onto the train, injuring the other thieves.

Quite by coincidence, on that very day Garfield was visiting a train museum in a town located at **54°54'N, 23°56'E**. This town was close to the site of the botched robbery. He got to the site just in time to watch the arrest of all four Diesel brothers.

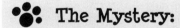 **The Mystery:**

Which one of the historic train robberies took place near the site of this botched attempt?

Name:_____

Geography Mysteries—Warm Up with Garfield

Imminent Eruptions

When Garfield goes to visit sites around the Ring of Fire, he's expecting to see fantastic circus acts with big cats leaping through burning rings. (Didn't he read the travel brochure?)

Instead, he stumbles into volcano territory. Everywhere he goes, things are rumbling and eruptions are imminent. On this particular day, he gets much too close to the mountain, and an eruption sends him running for his life.

🐾 The Mystery:

Which of these mountains could NOT be the one that's erupting during Garfield's trip to the Ring of Fire?

- MT. PINATUBO, PHILIPPINES
- EL CHICHÓN, MEXICO
- MT. ST. HELENS, OREGON, USA
- MT. BANDAI, JAPAN
- MT. LASSEN, CALIFORNIA, USA
- MT. KAMEN, RUSSIA
- MT. RUAPEHU, NEW ZEALAND
- MT. LLAIMA, CHILE
- MT. EREBUS, ANTARCTICA
- MT. ETNA, ITALY
- MT. ASKJA, ICELAND
- MT. KRAKATAU, INDONESIA
- KILAUEA, HAWAII, USA
- MT. SISHALDIN, ALEUTIAN ISLANDS

YIKES! A MAJOR HOTFOOT!

PANT

PANT

Name: _____

Cat Overboard

Garfield is fascinated to hear that the world is full of capes. He sets off to explore them.

He sails around these ten capes:

CAPE OF GOOD HOPE, CAPE HORN, CAPE SAN ANTONIO, CAPE COMORIN, CAPE MATAPAN, CAPE WRATH, CAPE ROCA, CAPE DEZHNEV, CAPE COD, AND CAPE MORRIS JESUP.

On one of the voyages, Garfield hovers too close to the bow of the ship and is washed overboard by a powerful wave. Luckily, a fishing boat spots his red cape, scoops him out of the water, and hangs him up to dry.

🐾 The Mystery:

Which of these bodies of water could NOT be the one from which Garfield is rescued?

- INDIAN OCEAN
- ATLANTIC OCEAN
- MEDITERRANEAN SEA
- PACIFIC OCEAN
- ARABIAN SEA
- TASMAN SEA
- CARIBBEAN SEA
- BERING STRAIT

Name:_____

SECONDS, PLEASE?

A Broken Promise

When Garfield went off to search for the tastiest doughnuts in the United States, he assured friends Odie, Jon, and Nermal that they could join him when he located the best ones. He never called. Instead, he lingered a while in each of the five states that had "to-die-for" doughnuts. Use the clues and the silhouettes to identify these states.

🐾 Clues:

1. The deepest canyon in the country is on its border, and it is home to the Sawtooth Mountains.

2. The state borders the Potomac River and has its landmass split by the Chesapeake Bay.

3. The mule is the state animal, and the state is home to the Gateway Arch.

4. This one ties with Missouri for the state with the most bordering neighbors.

5. A spot in this state is the geographical center of the contiguous 48 states.

🐾 The Mystery:

What are the five states where Garfield found the tastiest doughnuts? (Circle them.)

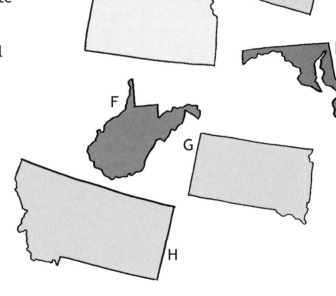

Name:_____

36

Run Aground

FREEZE-DRIED LASAGNA, DEAD AHEAD!

in the Archipelago

What luck! Each time Garfield visits an archipelago, some ship bearing a large load of food runs aground, spilling its cargo. Garfield usually offers to help with the recovery.

He has recovered:

• TONS OF CANNED ANCHOVIES IN TIERRA DEL FUEGO

• A SHIPMENT OF CHOCOLATE MARSHMALLOWS IN THE BAHAMAS

• A THOUSAND JARS OF PIZZA SAUCE IN THE AEGEAN ISLANDS

• A BOATLOAD OF SAUSAGES IN THE SOLOMON ISLANDS

• A CANISTER OF FROZEN SARDINE-CHEESE BALLS IN THE ALEUTIANS

🐾 The Mysteries:

Where has Garfield been when he has recovered these items? (Describe each location.)

Why might a ship run aground in or near an archipelago?

Name:_____

         Geography Mysteries—Warm Up with Garfield

Follow the Torch

Garfield manages to get invited to join the exclusive group of Olympic torchbearers. He carries the torch for a section of the European route (and stops often for the energizing snacks).

During this month, the torch is transported on foot and by truck

from *Lisbon, Portugal*

to *Bern, Switzerland*

to *Budapest, Hungary*

to *Sofia, Bulgaria*

to *Minsk, Belarus*

to *Tashkent, Uzbekistan*.

The torch travels by as direct a route as possible between cities.

The Mystery:

Through how many of these countries is the torch likely to pass on its journey?

PORTUGAL	CROATIA	BULGARIA	RUSSIA
BELARUS	ROMANIA	LITHUANIA	AUSTRIA
UZBEKISTAN	UKRAINE	KAZAKHSTAN	SERBIA
SPAIN	FRANCE	TURKMENISTAN	POLAND
SWITZERLAND	HUNGARY	BELGIUM	SLOVAKIA

Name:_____

38

The Spaghetti Sleuth

Jon takes Garfield to several foreign countries to see amazing human-built attractions. Garfield's first stop is always at an eatery to try out the local spaghetti (or whatever dish is closest to it).

> I CAN SEE CASTLES AND RUINS ANY TIME, BUT A DISH LIKE THIS IS A RARE EXPERIENCE

On this trip, Garfield's favorite dish and favorite attraction are found in the same country. This is the country (of all those they visit) that has the greatest number of neighbors (countries that border it).

They visit these attractions:

- THE SPHINX
- THE PANAMA CANAL
- BUCKINGHAM PALACE
- PRAGUE CASTLE
- TAJ MAHAL
- PERSEPOLIS
- CHICHEN ITZA RUINS
- PALACE OF VERSAILLES

The Mystery:

Which of these attractions is Garfield's favorite?

Name:_____

         Geography Mysteries—Warm Up with Garfield

A Noodle in a Haystack

An unusually clever jewel thief posed as a waiter in an exclusive Italian restaurant. When the power went out temporarily, she lifted a priceless pearl necklace from a wealthy diner, broke the string, and stuffed the pearls inside a tube of cheese manicotti (which is a large hollow noodle)!

Then this crafty crook took off in a small plane and dropped the noodle over a hayfield. She intended to retrieve the pearls when it was safe to do so.

Her plan was perfect—except for the cat. This waiter-thief-pilot did not know that Garfield would be napping on the other side of that haystack.

The thief did return to this dairy farm in a remote area near the southern end of the Gulf of Riga. But by then, the noodle had been eaten and the pearls had been turned over to the police.

 **The Mystery**

Where in the world is that haystack?

Name:_____

The Frozen Message

Cats have a way of picking up secrets. That's because most people think they can say anything in front of a cat, and it won't be understood or repeated. That is the case today. Garfield hears a group of shady characters bragging about their success in a holdup. They review their plans for stashing the cash in a remote location.

Garfield heads home to share the secret with Jon. He just stops for a bit to do a favorite activity—making a snow angel. The trouble is, by the time Jon finds him, Garfield is just about frozen and can't communicate anything. Jon has to thaw him out before Garfield can pass along the message he's got memorized.

 As he thaws, Garfield is able to give these clues he overheard:

THROUGH THE STRAIT OF MAGELLAN

ACROSS THE DRAKE PASSAGE

AT THE BASE OF MT. REX

 The Mystery:

Where are the robbers planning to hide the money?

Name:_____

41

The Melted Clues

NOW WHY DID I LEAVE THE POOL?

The lure of plentiful tropical foods brings Garfield and Jon south to the equator. Their vacation is interrupted by news that poachers have captured an endangered member of a cat species. Garfield just can't ignore the plight of a fellow cat. He leaves the cool poolside to help in the search.

LET'S HOPE THE POACHERS CONTINUE TO LEAVE A TRAIL OF FOOD

Many items are found at the site where the poachers waited to capture the cat. But no fingerprints are left because all the clues have melted in the intense heat: the chocolate bars, water jugs, plastic bags, packages of cheese, and containers of peanut butter.

It's a good thing Garfield is along, because a cat can sniff out another cat the way no human can. After lapping up the melted chocolate bars, cheese, and peanut butter, he picks up the scent and leads the search.

🐾 The Mystery:

Which of these could be the country where Garfield is searching?

TUVALU	LIBERIA
INDONESIA	KENYA
MALDIVES	COLOMBIA
PAPUA NEW GUINEA	EQUATORIAL GUINEA
GABON	ECUADOR
SOMALIA	UGANDA
KIRIBATI	

Name:_____

42

The Last Phone Call

TIO GATO'S COMADOR

Exhausted from his travels, Garfield decides to pursue the world's great dishes right from the comfort of his home— by using the phone.

He consults the Internet to make a list of numbers for restaurants around the world. He wants to find out if the food is promising enough to warrant a tasting trip. Garfield believes that he can get the best information about dishes by talking directly to the cooks.

Around noon on Monday (Garfield's home time, USA Eastern Standard Time), he places six calls. He gets answering machines, and leaves messages. All the cooks return his calls. The last call is the one that interests him most.

AH, SOUNDS LIKE THE PERFECT MEAL!

 Return calls
(Time is local for each city.)

Malolos, Philippines	at 6:20 AM Tues
Kihei, Hawaii	at 7:15 PM Mon
Timaru, New Zealand	at 7 AM Tues
Mercedes, Uruguay	at 6 PM Mon
Toliara, Madagascar	at 8 AM Tues
Santa Ana, El Salvador	at 5:30 PM Mon

The Mystery:

From what location is the last call and at what time does Garfield receive it?

Name:_____

The Misplaced Mummies

Something is wrong in Giza Square. Mummies are missing. The authorities are always alert for culprits trying to steal mummies, so they cannot have been removed from the square. But clearly, mummies of two queens, two nobles, and one of the royal children are not where they belong.

Clues have been left behind—clues which seem to indicate that the mummies are still in the area:

- beneath royal barge, southeast corner of Khufu's tomb
- beside the noble's tomb farthest west of the Sphinx
- behind easternmost Menkaure's queen tomb
- behind farthest west child's tomb
- behind Valley Temple east of Khafre's queen

🐾 The Mystery:

Where are the mummies?
(Circle the locations.)

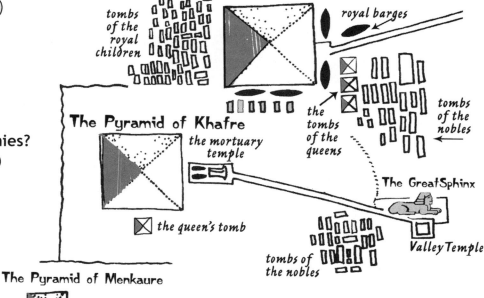

Giza

The Great Pyramid of Khufu

tombs of the royal children

royal barges

the tombs of the queens

tombs of the nobles

The Pyramid of Khafre

the mortuary temple

The Great Sphinx

☒ the queen's tomb

tombs of the nobles

Valley Temple

The Pyramid of Menkaure

the mortuary temple

83 Valley Temple

☒☒☒ the tombs of the queens

N W E S

Name:_____

The Post-it® Bandit

Garfield researches and plans carefully for his upcoming trip to the Eastern Hemisphere. He uses Post-it® notes to mark the map with the attractions he wants to see.

Here's his list:

His plans are foiled when someone sneaks in during his nap, steals two notes, replaces them with blanks, and rearranges some of the others.

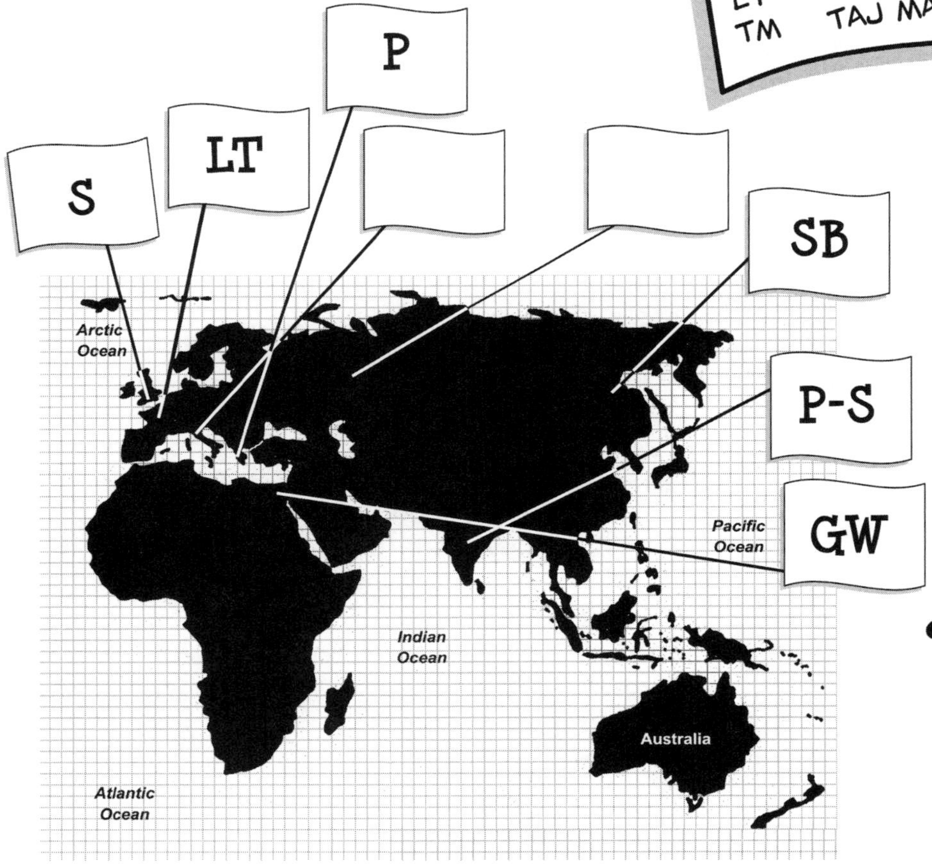

SB	ST. BASIL'S CATHEDRAL
ET	EIFFEL TOWER
GW	GREAT WALL
P-S	PYRAMIDS AND SPHINX
P	PARTHENON
S	STONEHENGE
LT	LEANING TOWER OF PISA
TM	TAJ MAHAL

The Mysteries:

Which Post-it® notes are missing, and where do they belong?

How many of the notes are still correctly placed?

Name:_____

A Furious Chase

When a quick-fingered tourist snatches Garfield's cellphone
in Luxembourg, the spunky cat is not about to let her get away.
After all, that phone has the numbers of the most important pizza,
taco, burger, and hot dog shops in Garfield's life!

Garfield hops on his bike in hot pursuit of the thief.
To retrieve that phone, he rides several days and travels
(by land or boat):

- over flat-topped hills,
- in and out of deep narrow valleys with steep sides,
- along coastlines that jut out into water,
- through dry sandy regions,
- over steep mounds of sand,
- along narrow strips of land that connect two larger bodies of land,
- along small rivers that flow into larger rivers, and
- around areas where rivers empty into lakes.

THIS IS ONE SEARCH THAT CAN'T BE PHONED IN!

🐾 The Mystery:

Which of these landforms or water forms
are NOT encountered in his pursuit?

STRAIT	TRIBUTARY	DUNE
FJORD	OASIS	MOUTH
CAPE	MESA	DESERT
CANYON	ISTHMUS	GULF

Name:_____

The Phony Alibi

Swiss chocolate is rumored to be the finest in the world, so as soon as he gets off the plane, Garfield heads straight to the nearest chocolate shop. He arrives on a Tuesday afternoon in July, just before the 6:00 PM closing time. Oh no! Just moments before that, the shop was robbed. All the chocolates are gone!!

By the next morning, the police are questioning a chocolate-covered suspect. Garfield can't resist joining the investigation. (The reward for an arrest might be chocolate.) Evidence consists of chocolate on clothing and chocolaty fingerprints at the scene. But the suspect has an alibi from a friend from Perth, Australia.

Garfield listens to the alibi, and assures the police that the friend's statement is a lie.

CHESTER COULD NOT HAVE ROBBED THAT SHOP. HE WAS ON THE PHONE WITH ME AT EXACTLY THAT TIME. I REMEMBER THAT I WAS JUST FEEDING MY KIDS AN EARLY BREAKFAST WHEN THE CALL CAME AT WHAT WOULD HAVE BEEN 5:30 TO 6:30 PM IN SWITZERLAND. SCHOOL IS OUT FOR SUMMER VACATION, AND WE WERE GETTING READY TO GO OFF AND SPEND THE DAY AT THE BEACH. CHESTER AND I TALKED FOR AN HOUR.

 **The Mystery:**

How does Garfield know that the alibi is phony?

Name: _____

Trouble at the Hotel

Garfield is having some unwelcome trouble checking into the hotel. After a long trip, he and Jon are interested in one thing: getting into a room and getting to sleep.

Their journey of many hours brings them to a country that:

• IS FARTHER WEST THAN THE PHILIPPINES

• IS FARTHER EAST THAN INDIA

• IS FARTHER NORTH THAN MALAYSIA

• IS FARTHER SOUTH THAN BHUTAN

• BORDERS THE GULF OF THAILAND

• DOES NOT BORDER THE SOUTH CHINA SEA

• DOES NOT BORDER THE BAY OF BENGAL

 **The Mystery:**

Where in the world is this hotel?

Name:_____

The Undelivered Postcards

I HOPE THEY ALL WRITE BACK!

List of Postcards Sent

1. ENGLAND
2. BOSNIA
3. KUWAIT
4. NORTH KOREA
5. DENMARK
6. OMAN
7. BORNEO
8. SENEGAL
9. TRINIDAD AND TOBAGO
10. BELIZE
11. BANGLADESH
12. MONGOLIA
13. GRENADA
14. HAITI
15. SURINAME
16. NEW CALEDONIA

Garfield continues his never-ending search for great food around the world. He sends postcards to restaurants in each of these world regions requesting information and recipes:

North and Central America
South America
Eastern Europe
Western Europe
Africa
Northern Asia
The Middle East
Southwestern Asia
Southeast Asia
Oceania

Unfortunately, every fourth postcard on Garfield's list never reaches its destination. Fortunately, many delicious food pictures and ideas are sent back to him.

 The Mystery:

How many of the world's regions are NOT reached by one or more of Garfield's postcards?

Name:_____

Geography Mysteries—Warm Up with Garfield

The Itinerary Mix-up

Garfield is off to Scotland and the island of Ireland, with his itineraries in hand. As usual, he has made a list of things he wants to see and do at each location. But something is wrong with the lists!

in Ireland . . .

1. Eat Irish Stew in Belfast
2. Visit Cape Clear
3. Take pictures of Giant's Causeway
4. Eat fruitcake in Glasgow
5. Swim in St. George's Channel
6. Eat pancakes in Londonderry
7. Hunt for the Loch Ness Monster
8. Sail on the North Sea
9. See the dungeon at Blarney Castle
10. Jet ski on Lough Neagh

in Scotland . . .

1. Eat mashed potatoes in Dublin
2. Sail to the Hebrides Islands
3. Find pizza in Edinburgh
4. Eat Scotch pies in Aberdeen
5. Swim in Donegal Bay
6. Drink coffee in the coffee shop where J.K. Rowling began writing the Harry Potter books
7. Read limericks in the town of Limerick
8. See the Firth of Fourth

The Mystery:

Which items are on the wrong list?

Name:_____

Geography Mysteries—Warm Up with Garfield　　　50

Pursuit of a Pizza Substitute

THIS COULD USE SOME PIZZA SAUCE

Pizza is no doubt a favorite food of Garfield's. He'll eat any kind anywhere. When he hears about the Middle Eastern flatbreads such as lavash and pita, he thinks they sound a lot like pizza dough.

Garfield makes a list of countries to visit, then follows his stomach—having a great time eating his way around the Middle East.

The Mystery:

What countries does Garfield visit that are NOT on his list?

Garfield's list:

Afghanistan
Iran
Kuwait
Yemen
Saudi Arabia
Iraq
Israel

Garfield's Trip:

. . . .

Countries of the Middle East

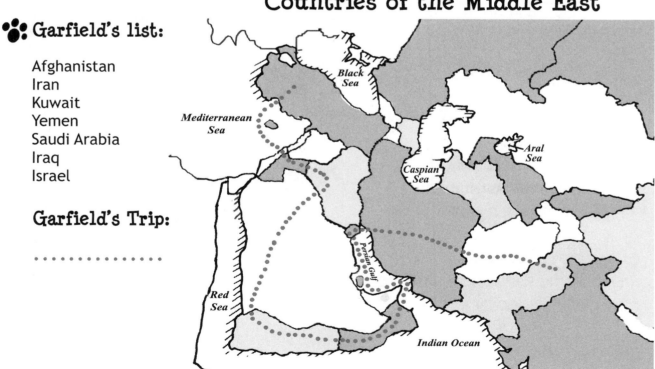

Name:_____

The Tough Question

It's geography-bee season. Garfield finds himself, once again, in the semifinal round. This is one of the toughest questions he has had to answer in all his geography-bee experience.

Will Garfield still be in the bee when he's done with this question? Garfield has been to all of these countries. Did he pay as much attention to the geography as he did to the food?

The Question:

Which of these countries has the greatest number of neighbors sharing a border?

INDIA
GUATEMALA
BOTSWANA
AFGHANISTAN
MACEDONIA
ROMANIA
CÔTE D'IVOIRE
PARAGUAY
SLOVAKIA
DEMOCRATIC REPUBLIC OF THE CONGO
BOLIVIA
IRAN

Garfield's Answer:
Democratic Republic of the Congo

The Mystery:

Is Garfield's answer correct?

Name:_____

Extreme Conditions

Garfield is on the hunt again. This time it's a search for a stolen formula. Only the top scientists at the Rola Cola factory know how to make this top-selling drink. The formula is kept locked in a heavy vault except for those few moments each month when the scientists refresh their memories before mixing up a new batch. But now it is missing. The cola company owners must get it back before the thieves can figure out how to read and copy the electronic file.

This extreme emergency calls for extreme measures. Garfield tracks the thieves by GPS, and parachutes into locations where they might be found. They make the chase more interesting (and challenging) by hiding out in locations with some of the world's most extreme conditions.

A SURPRISE ATTACK IS MY FORMULA FOR SUCCESS!

Garfield drops into countries (or other places) where these can be found:

1. the coldest temperature ever recorded
2. the hottest temperature ever recorded
3. the longest cave system in the world
4. the deepest cave in the world
5. the wettest spot in the world
6. the driest spot in the world
7. the longest fjord in the world
8. the windiest spot ever recorded

🐾 The Mystery:

Into what places does Garfield's search take him?

Name:_____

The Uninvited Guest

Jon and Garfield are repeatedly surprised (and annoyed) by a pesky crab that joins in on their vacation. This crab shows up everywhere they go.

- When they explore the spit, the crab is right on their heels.
- When they cross the lagoon, the crab squeezes between them.
- When they play on the sandbar, the crab wants to play along.
- When they climb on a stack, the crab is waiting for them.
- When they relax on the beach, the crab relaxes beside them.
- When they watch the sea life around a reef, the crab watches them.
- When they sail around an atoll, the crab is on the bow of the boat.
- When they surf in the gulf, the crab clings to Jon's surfboard.

The crab turns up in all their trip photos, except one: the one that includes a formation of resistant rock left standing after softer rock is worn away.

The Mystery:

What shoreline feature is shown in the photo without the crab?

Name:_____

The Backward Mystery

Champ the Bobcat is the revered mascot of Montana State University. When his mascot uniform is stolen during a break-in at the athletic department, the entire state is up in arms.

To avoid being caught, the thief poses as a real bobcat and criss-crosses the USA on airplanes. His luck runs out when he steps off a plane in Lexington, Kentucky. He runs right into Garfield; and Garfield knows a phony cat when he sees one.

Eventually, authorities piece together the thief's escape route.

- The thief is apprehended in Kentucky at 8 PM on Friday as he gets off a flight that had left Alaska at 9 AM (Alaska time).

- Before the flight, he spent 10 hours in Alaska.

- He flew to Alaska from Hawaii, spending 4 hours in the air.

- Before that, he was in Hawaii for 2 hours.

- He left Arizona at noon (Arizona time) and flew 7 hours to Hawaii.

- He was in Arizona for 12 hours.

- He got to Arizona by traveling 6 hours from Virginia.

- He spent 2 hours in Virginia.

- Two hours after the theft was discovered, he left Montana for a 5-hour flight to Virginia.

 The Mysteries:

When was the theft discovered? (Write the time and day.)

When did the thief arrive in Arizona (Arizona time and day)?

Name:_____

Geography Mysteries—Warm Up with Garfield

The Lure of the Islands

How can Garfield possibly resist a visit to a place named the South Sandwich Islands? He can't! He sees an ad in a travel magazine and gets himself there as quickly as possible.

> THIS IS MY FAVORITE KIND OF SANDWICH.

The Mystery:

Which of these probably are NOT true about Garfield's location?

1. He's in a small chain of eight islands.
2. The islands are owned by Great Britain.
3. He's just off the coast of Georgia, USA.
4. The islands are bordered by the Atlantic Ocean.
5. He's just north of Cuba.
6. The islands have rugged mountains.
7. South America is the closest continent.
8. The islands are bordered by the Scotia Bay.
9. He's close to the equator.
10. There are dozens of sandwich shops on the islands.

Name:_____

56

A Fortune in the Sand Trap

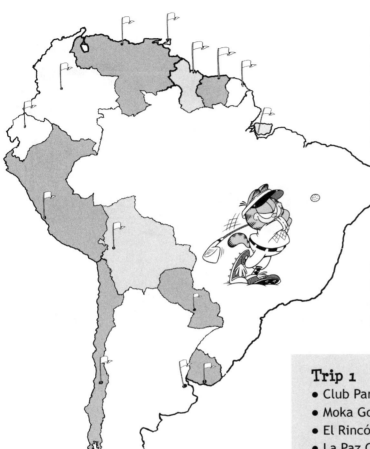

Once again, Garfield goes undercover in the sports world—this time to search for stolen objects worth a fortune. A prize collection of pure gold golf balls disappeared from a museum. Rumor has it that someone fled to South America and actually played with these treasured items. The crook was a lousy golfer, so now the golden golf balls are stuck in a sand trap on some golf course somewhere on the continent.

Garfield takes two trips to South America to search, playing golf at these courses (in this order). Draw his route on the map for each trip.

Trip 1
- Club Paramaribo in Paramaribo, Suriname
- Moka Golf Course in Maraval, Trinidad
- El Rincón Gulf Club in Bogota, Colombia
- La Paz Golf Course in La Paz, Bolivia
- Quito Tennis and Golf Club in Quito, Ecuador
- Lima Golf Course in Lima, Peru

Trip 2
- Club de Golf Los Leones in Santiago, Chile
- Lagunita Country Club in Caracas, Venezuela
- Golf del Cerro in Montevideo, Uruguay
- Praia do Paiva in Recife, Brazil
- Carlos Franco Country Club in Asuncion, Paraguay
- Valle Arriba Golf Course in Caracas, Venezuela

 **The Mystery:**

Garfield finds the golden golf balls in the country where the routes of the two trips intersect. On what golf course are the golden balls caught in the sand trap?

Name:_____

Fries Extraordinaire

Ahhhh! After many tries, Garfield finds what he deems to be the best French fries in the world. (Not surprisingly, this is in a town in southern France.) He keeps going back to the restaurant for more. One day, to his dismay, he learns that the chef has been lured away to another country. What's worse: There are different reports as to the chef's new location.

TRÉS SUBLIME!

Garfield follows up on all the leads, going to many cities and tasting piles of fries as he goes. He gets waylaid in four cities, because the fries come so close to perfection. In the end, he decides to keep eating fries and not worry about finding that chef.

1 CITY ON THE PREGOLYA RIVER JUST UPSTREAM FROM FRISCHES LAGOON

2 CITY FARTHEST SOUTH ON THE TIP OF THE ISTRIA PENINSULA

🐾 The Mystery:

What are the four places where Garfield gets waylaid by the excellent fries?

4 CITY THAT LIES IN TWO EUROPEAN COUNTRIES, SPLIT BY THE DANUBE RIVER

3 TOWN FARTHEST SOUTHEAST IN THE BRITISH ISLES

Name:_____

58

The Grass Skirt Incident

Garfield steals the show wherever he goes. His hula dancing act is so spectacular and unusual that he's invited to perform all over Polynesia (and beyond).

OOPS!

In fact, his popularity sparks jealousy among some other dancers. Competition becomes so intense that someone switches the grass skirts backstage before a performance. This leaves Garfield to perform in a skirt that falls off when his hips begin to undulate. Imagine his humiliation!

Garfield performs on these islands:

- New Zealand
- French Polynesia
- Barbados
- Pitcairn Islands

- Vanuatu
- Cook Islands
- Samoa
- Channel Islands

- Elba
- Phoenix Islands
- Christmas Island

- Line Islands
- Tonga
- Tuvalu

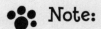 **The Mystery:**

Which of the performance locations could NOT be the place where the embarrassing incident took place?

Note:

Never fear—Garfield is not easily intimidated. He continues the show, finishes the tour, and is more popular than ever!

Name:_____

59

Strange Stories

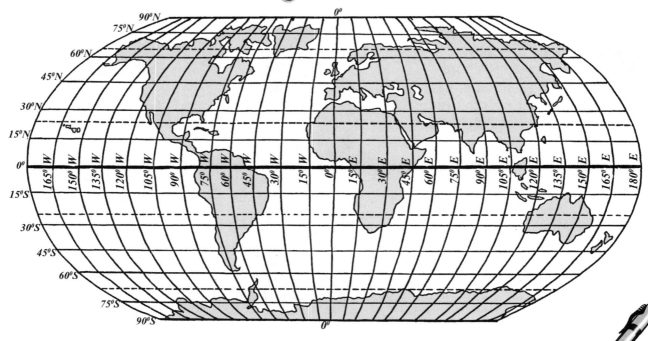

The job of a reporter is to get an unusual story—hopefully before anyone else gets it. Garfield's natural curiosity drives him to jet all over the world, finding out about strange events. As he does this, he counts the number of times he crosses key lines of latitude and longitude.

Here are the stories he investigates (in this order.) Letter(s) after each story show the direction(s) he travels to the next location.

🐾 The Mystery:

How many times does Garfield cross each of these as he travels to get the six stories (starting in the country of the first story)?

___ Arctic Circle   ___ Antarctic Circle

___ Tropic of Cancer   ___ Tropic of Capricorn

___ Equator   ___ Prime Meridian

___ International Date Line

🐾 The Stories

1) hundreds of enchiladas found wrapped in $100 bills in Guatemala (W & S)

2) baby gorilla lost in southern Gabon (N & E)

3) climbers held captive by abominable snowmen in the Himalayan Mountains of southern Tibet (W & S)

4) a two-year-old charming snakes on the southern tip of Argentina (W & N)

5) 80-foot popsicle in Northern Greenland (E & S)

6) lake once on fire in southern Finland

I'LL TRAVEL ANYWHERE FOR THE "MEWS" OF THE DAY!

Name:_____

Imposters on Parade

Garfield proudly leads one of the best marching bands in the world as it tours the capital cities of several nations. But the good time is spoiled by crime when some imposters (who are also crooks) join the parade in one city.

Unbeknownst to Garfield and most of the band members, some thieves rent uniforms and join the band as a way of moving stolen musical instruments through the streets of the city without being noticed.

These are the capitals where the parades are held:

- WELLINGTON
  - JAKARTA
    - ANTANANARIVO
      - BUENOS AIRES
        - MUMBAI
          - MASERU
            - SUVA
              - KUALA LUMPUR
                - SANTIAGO
                  - COLOMBO

SOME OF THESE BAND MEMBERS DON'T LOOK FAMILIAR!

One of these cities is the national capital that is farthest south in the world. The parade that is infiltrated by imposters takes place in another capital (listed above) closest in latitude to the southernmost capital.

🐾 The Mystery:

Where is the parade that is troubled by imposters?
(city and country)

Name:_____

The Bumpy Flights

The travelers are already feeling cramped and grumpy from the long trip. Three stretches of heavy turbulence make them even more uncomfortable.

Each time, the pilot apologizes for the shaking and swaying of the plane, explaining that turbulence is common when flying over mountain ranges. This turbulence occurs when they have just left Mexico City, heading east, and again after a stop in Rabat, Morocco, when they head east out over the Sahara Desert.

The third time they experience turbulence is when they cross from the European section of Russia into the Asian part of the country.

This time, the annoyance turns to excitement. The bumps and thumps shake open an overhead bin, and out spills a 20-gallon container of jelly beans. All of a sudden, Garfield becomes a fan of air turbulence.

 The Mystery:

What mountain ranges are they crossing when they feel the turbulence each time?

Name:_____

62

Million-Dollar Fish

A group of jewel thieves escapes by boat after lifting millions of dollars worth of emeralds from a high-security museum in Venice. As they head out to sea, the Italian Guardia Costiera (Coast Guard) is suddenly on their tail. One thief panics and drops four of the jewels overboard. Floating down into the water, the shiny emeralds attract the attention of sea creatures—who swallow them up.

Since Garfield is an expert on fish behavior, he helps out with the search. The Guardia Costiera hopes that Garfield's keen senses will lead him to the creatures with emeralds in their tummies.

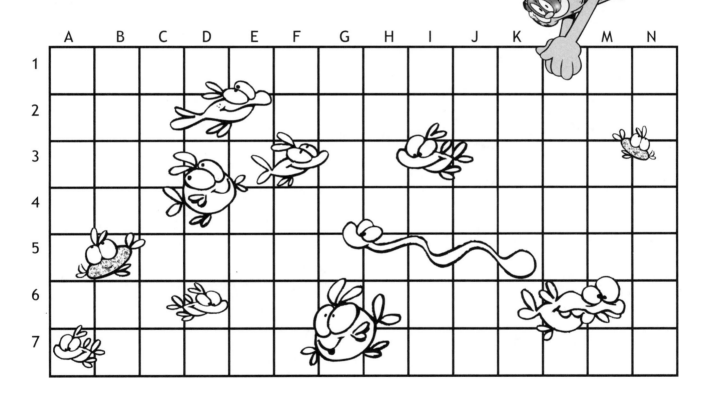

 It doesn't take Garfield long to solve the mystery. He identifies the creatures at these locations on the grid:

In F3   In M2, N2, M3, and N3

In A5 and B5   In L6 and M6

 **The Mystery:**

Which creatures swallowed the emeralds? (Color them.)

Name:_____

The Undercover Waiter

Garfield frequently goes undercover as a waiter at a fancy restaurant. This makes it easy for him to eavesdrop on conversations, pick up clues, follow suspects, and gather information on all sorts of mysteries. He has been to several places in this disguise:

- on an island where some people speak Papiamento
- in a country that has 14 sheep for every person
- in the largest city north of the Arctic Circle
- in a country that is home to the Aswan Dam
- in a city that used to be named Saigon
- in the smallest country in the world
- in every national capital located on the Danube River

ENJOY!

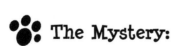 **The Mystery:**

Where has Garfield been (as an undercover waiter)?

Name:_____

64

Purloined Pepperoni

There's excitement in the house when Garfield hears that seven groups of pepperoni fans around the world are competing to make the world's longest pepperoni.

There's horror in the house when Garfield learns that all seven of the record-breaking pepperonis have been stolen. Disappearing pepperoni is serious business to Garfield, and he's eager to help.

Garfield follows the distinctive scent and retrieves the missing record-breaking pepperonis in these locations:

- 35°S, 71°W
- 12°N, 85°W
- 7°N, 134°E
- 13°S, 17°E
- 53°N, 106°W
- 40°N, 59°E
- 5°S, 101°E

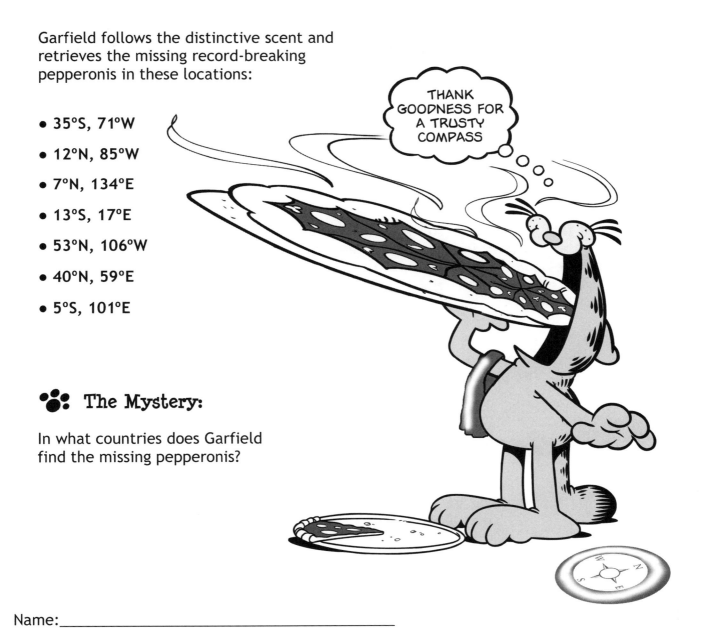

THANK GOODNESS FOR A TRUSTY COMPASS

🐾 The Mystery:

In what countries does Garfield find the missing pepperonis?

Name:_____

Intrigue in the Indies

Nothing thrills Jon quite like an island vacation. When he has a chance to spend a week in the West Indies, he grabs Garfield and heads for the beaches. While Jon relaxes, Garfield gets caught up in the intrigue of piracy in the area.

News has it that a band of pirates has been circulating through the 2,000-mile-long chain of islands. They boldly rob food from yachts as the ships are docked for the night.

Reports of missing goods come in from

- Eleuthera
- Caicos
- eastern Cuba
- the Dominican Republic
- Puerto Rico
- Barbados
- St. Kitts

Authorities notice a pattern in the path of the pirates. Based on this, they make some assumptions about where the pirates will strike next.

🐾 The Mystery:

Which of these islands is likely to be the pirates' next stop: Jamaica, St. Croix, St. Lucia, Grand Cayman, or Haiti?

Name:

66

Geo-Clues

NEXT CASE!

It's a good thing he keeps brushed up on geography, because Judge Garfield needs it to decide these cases. He hears each accusation brought by the prosecution, listens to the defense, and makes a ruling.

Judge Garfield presiding

CASE 1: Piracy in the Caribbean

Prosecution claims that Slick Sam chased down several ships with his fast yacht and robbed them during the week of September 4–10.

Defense insists Sam was not even using his boat during that time, because it had been damaged in a severe typhoon that stuck off the coast of Cuba on September 3.

Ruling: for the prosecution

CASE 2: Penguin Poachers

Prosecution accuses Nadia and Inga of killing penguins in the Barents Sea off the coast of Arctic Russia.

Defense argues that the two friends have never been to the Barents Sea and have never harmed penguins or any other birds.

Ruling: for the defense

CASE 3: The Shifty Stargazer

Prosecution charges Lucy with stealing telescopes at a stargazing party in Costa Rica. Prosecutors say she lifted the goods while stargazers were awed by the colorful aurora borealis display.

Defense says Lucy was at the party, but did nothing other than enjoy the stars.

Ruling: for the defense

CASE 4: The Maquiladora Alibi

Prosecution charges that Carlos passed forged checks to banks in his hometown of Málaga, Spain, during the month of July.

Defense says Carlos was working during banking hours every day that month. His job, they say, is assembling coffee grinders at the local maquiladora.

Ruling: for the prosecution

 The Mystery: Why does Garfield confidently make each of these rulings?

Name:_____

The Cover-up

Soccer matches are notoriously rowdy, especially in parts of the world where soccer is the national obsession. Some gangs of clever pickpockets take advantage of this. They synchronize their watches and lift wallets, jewelry, and purses at the same moment. Then they start fights throughout the stadium to cover up the thefts. This allows them to get away unnoticed.

As Garfield assists in the investigation, he manages to get invited to warm up with the players for several matches. He's on the field with these home teams:

REAL MADRID (SPAIN)

AL ORUBA (OMAN)

ATLANTE (CANCUN, MEXICO)

FC PORTO (PORTUGAL)

OLYMPIAKOS (GREECE)

KELANTAN (MALAYSIA)

AGF (DENMARK)

KALMAR FF (SWEDEN)

AL AHLY CAIRO (EGYPT)

GET READY FOR IT!

🐾 The Mystery:

Which of these peninsulas does Garfield visit during this investigation?

- Indian
- Yucatan
- Balkan
- Malay
- Jutland
- Sinai
- Baja
- Scandinavian
- Korean
- Colaba
- Iberian
- Musandam

GOOOOAL!

Name:_____

Distress in the Desert

Whatever possessed Garfield to sign up for a tour of the world's deserts? Well, he thought the travel agent said he'd be getting a wonderful selection of the world's great *desserts!*

Now, here he is, distressed in the desert—looking for an oasis, and seeing the occasional dessert mirage.

Garfield is in a subtropical desert somewhere between 30°N latitude and 30°S latitude.

 ### The Mystery:

Which of these deserts might Garfield be touring?

- MOJAVE
- SAHARA
- ATACAMA
- NAMIB
- CHIHUAHUAN
- KALAHARI
- GOBI
- ARABIAN
- PATAGONIA
- GREAT SANDY
- ARCTIC
- IRANIAN

Name:_____

 Geography Mysteries—Warm Up with Garfield

The Decoys

A thief with a sweet tooth planned a robbery with a clever escape. At a jelly bean factory in San Francisco, she gathered up all the blueberry jelly beans in a huge bag. Then she hopped onto a plane headed for southern California.

Over Eureka, she jumped out of the plane and landed in the sand dunes (where she had stashed a motorcycle). Two friends with motorcycles and large bags also waited in the dunes. She and the two decoys took off in different directions.

The thief took the route that crossed, passed, or followed these features: the Appalachian Mountains, the Coastal Mountains, the Sierra Nevada Range, Mt. Whitney, the Coastal Plains, the Central Valley, the Everglades, the Rio Grande River, and the Mojave Desert. Garfield caught up with her at the end of her route.

 ## The Mystery:

Where did Garfield catch the jelly bean thief: on the shores of the Straits of Mackinac, on the shores of Lake Okeechobee, or on the shores of Delaware Bay?

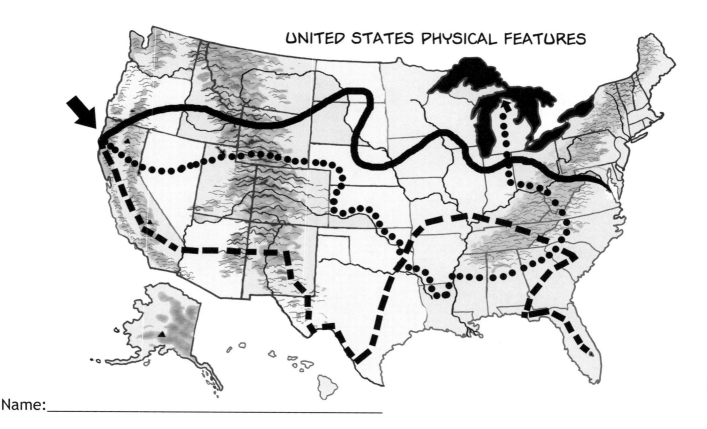

UNITED STATES PHYSICAL FEATURES

Name:_____

Disturbance at the Bee

Bees descended on the room where the geography bee was underway. Chaos broke out. All the answers were being shouted out but weren't matched to any questions.

1. Is more or less than half of Africa in the southern hemisphere?

2. The war in Vietnam spread to what two neighboring countries?

3. Where did thousands of people move in 1848 in hopes of finding gold?

4. What country controls the Panama Canal?

5. What city is sacred to Jews, Christians, and Muslims?

6. What are the two official languages of Canada?

7. Where was a wall built to divide east from west?

8. Shinto is a religion of what country?

 The Mystery:

Which answers are NOT correct for any of the questions?

U.S.   **Panama**   Japan   China

BERLIN   *CANADIAN*   French

ENGLISH   MORE   LESS

Jerusalem   AFRICA   LONDON

CALIFORNIA   LAOS   **INDIA**   Cambodia

Name:_____

Switched Suitcases

OH NO! NOT THE ANCHOVIES!

In a crowded airport, someone switches suitcases with Garfield. Is it an accident? Or is it the scent of those anchovies in Garfield's suitcase that lured someone (maybe another cat) to steal it? Whatever the reason, he is missing his prized possessions!

Although the suitcases are identical in kind, the stickers show that the two travelers have been to different places.

🐾 The Mystery:

What country or countries have both travelers visited?

Mt. Elbert

Angkor Wat

Khyber Pass

MT. FUJI

Brandenburg Gate

Sydney Opera House

Holy See

THE OUTBACK

PILLARS OF HERCULES

Okefenokee Swamp

Land of Fire & Ice

TRANSYLVANIA

Name:_____

72

The Refrigerator Theft

It was probably foolish of Garfield to take the whole refrigerator on his Mediterranean cruise. It was just too much of a temptation for food-loving thieves. And so, somewhere between the coast of Syria and the island of Cypress, it happened: The refrigerator was hijacked.

A fast boat took off, heading for the coast of Turkey. Garfield watched in agony as the refrigerator sped away. Before long, however, he was in hot (and hungry) pursuit.

Luckily, he could intercept the thieves' communications and hear where they were going. He heard them describe their route by sea from

TURKEY TO CRETE
TO MONTENEGRO
TO TUNISIA
TO MALLORCA
TO MONACO
TO SARDINIA
TO MOROCCO.

He followed, traveling these directions: southwest, northwest, south and east, northwest, northeast, southwest, and southwest again.

 ## The Mystery:

Did Garfield travel in the right directions to stay on the trail of the refrigerator?

Name:_____

Lost in Lost Valley

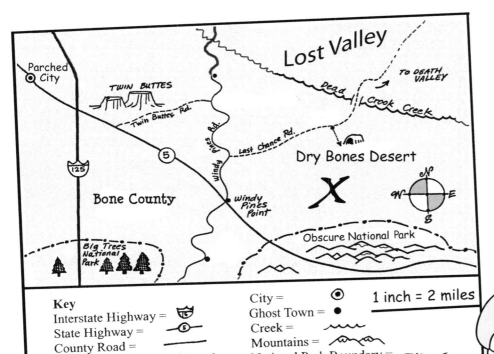

Garfield didn't think he needed to bother with a map when he went to visit some old ghost towns. That explains why he is now lost in Lost Valley. (See the X on the map for his location.)

He wanders north across Last Chance Road to Dead Crook Creek, northwest along the creek, and south on Windy Pines Road to Red Valley.

From there he heads directly west through the national park until he hits Highway 125. Here he catches a ride to Parched City, where a worried Jon is waiting for him.

 **The Mystery:**

What is the total distance Garfield walks or rides from the X marked on the map to Parched City? (Circle one.)

about 1 to 5 mi   about 16 to 20 mi
about 6 to 10 mi   about 21 to 25 mi
about 11 to 15 mi   about 26 to 30 mi

Name:_____

The Hasty Leap

I LOVE TO MAKE A SPLASH

Garfield shows off his cannonball form at lakes all over the world. Today he is taking the leap into one of the world's great lakes, without stopping to check the water conditions. (This is a bad idea, Garfield!) Let's hope he is not jumping into Boiling Lake!

This particular lake is in a country that borders a sea, a large gulf, and an ocean. It is located south of the Tropic of Cancer. It is one of the lakes Garfield has on his list:

LAKE SUPERIOR

LAKE NIOS

LAKE MARICAIBO

LAKE BAIKAL

BOILING LAKE

LAKE CHAPALA

LAKE TANGANYIKA

LAKE TEXCOCO

LAKE TITICACA

LAKE VICTORIA

LAKE TAHOE

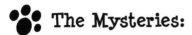 The Mysteries:

Which could be the lake (or lakes) for this jump?

Which of these lakes has actually exploded?

Name:_____

Geography Mysteries—Warm Up with Garfield

Trouble on the Ice

As Garfield is enjoying a leisurely afternoon of skating on a frozen river, trouble erupts. Some prankster whizzes by and grabs his hat. Garfield races after the culprit. A crash ensues, and the trouble leads to a hospital emergency room in the nearest town.

Garfield's skating fiasco takes place at approximately this location:

41°38'N, 72°3'W

I MAY BE ON CRUTCHES, BUT AT LEAST I GOT MY HAT BACK!

The Mysteries:

On what river is Garfield skating?

Is this north of the Arctic Circle?

What town is probably the place where the hospital is located?

Name:_____

76

The Great Hamburger Search

Guess what happens after Garfield reads an article titled **"15 Hamburgers You Must Eat Before You Die"**? Right! He decides he must try every one of them!

Here are the restaurants on the list. Garfield travels to every one of these cities and tests all the burgers—some of them more than once.

- Le Tub in Hollywood, FL
- Dick's Drive-In in Seattle, WA
- Penguin Drive-In in Charlotte, NC
- Billy Goat Tavern in Chicago, IL
- Ted's Montana Grill in Atlanta, GA
- Bobcat Bite in Las Vegas, NV
- Louis' Lunch in New Haven, CT
- Burger Joint in San Francisco, CA

- Cherry Cricket in Denver, CO
- Rouge in Philadelphia, PA
- Peter Luger Steak House in Brooklyn, NY
- Keller's Drive-In in Dallas, TX
- Arctic Roadrunner in Anchorage, AK
- Redrum Burger Drive-In in Davis, CA
- Port of Call in New Orleans, LA

 The Mystery: How many of these hamburgers are found in capital cities?

Name:_____

         Geography Mysteries—Warm Up with Garfield

Time Trickery

When they stop to think about it, Garfield and Jon realize that time travel actually is possible. They can jump backward or forward a whole day, just by crossing the International Date Line. Remembering this, Garfield decides to try it.

- He leaves Samoa at noon on Sunday, traveling one hour to Tonga.

- He leaves Tonga at 5:00 PM on Tuesday and flies three hours to eastern Australia.

- He leaves Australia at 11:00 AM on Thursday and flies three hours to Fiji.

- He leaves Fiji at 9:00 AM on Saturday and flies four hours to Hawaii.

 The Mysteries:

When does Garfield arrive in Tonga?

When does Garfield arrive in Australia?

When does Garfield arrive in Fiji?

When does Garfield arrive in Hawaii?

(Give a time and day as the solution to each mystery.)

Name:_____

Shocking News

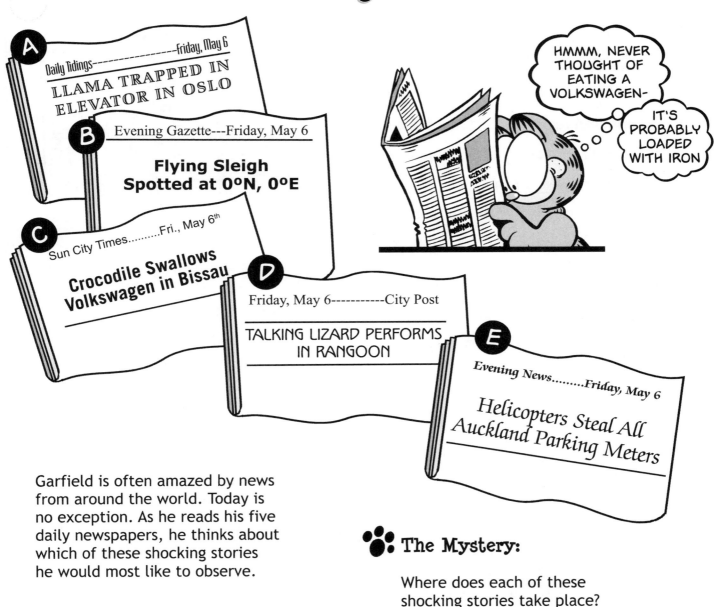

A — Daily Tidings — Friday, May 6
LLAMA TRAPPED IN ELEVATOR IN OSLO

B — Evening Gazette --- Friday, May 6
Flying Sleigh Spotted at 0°N, 0°E

C — Sun City Times .... Fri., May 6th
Crocodile Swallows Volkswagen in Bissau

D — Friday, May 6 ----------- City Post
TALKING LIZARD PERFORMS IN RANGOON

E — Evening News .... Friday, May 6
Helicopters Steal All Auckland Parking Meters

HMMM, NEVER THOUGHT OF EATING A VOLKSWAGEN—

IT'S PROBABLY LOADED WITH IRON

Garfield is often amazed by news from around the world. Today is no exception. As he reads his five daily newspapers, he thinks about which of these shocking stories he would most like to observe.

The Mystery:

Where does each of these shocking stories take place?

Name:_____

Geography Mysteries—Warm Up with Garfield

History Mysteries

Geography plays a huge role in world history.
Garfield can match up the countries with
these history mysteries. Can you?

____ **A.** disputed region in 1982 Argentina-UK war

____ **B.** country formed as a British penal colony

____ **C.** island center of Minoan culture

____ **D.** location of missile storage that sparked 1962
dispute between the U.S. and the USSR

____ **E.** site of first modern Olympic games

____ **F.** members of 1994 NAFTA agreement

____ **G.** country split at end of war in 1953

____ **H.** site of famous 16th-century ceiling painting

The Mystery:

What country or place name
(and number on the map)
solves each mystery?

Name:_____

Hooked on Travel

Fishing has immediate rewards—especially for a fishing expert like Garfield. Because he always wants to hook more interesting and tasty rewards, Garfield tries out some of the world's greatest rivers:

AMAZON

YANGTZE

DANUBE

EUPHRATES

GANGES

MACKENZIE

INDUS

NILE

OB

MISSISSIPPI

A RIVER HAS SOMETHING IN COMMON WITH ME —A BIG MOUTH

 The Mystery:

When Garfield visits the mouth of each of the rivers on the list, which of the bodies of water below is he NOT LIKELY to see?

Atlantic Ocean	East China Sea	Black Sea
Persian Gulf	Bay of Bengal	Arctic Sea
Mediterranean Sea	Gulf of Mexico	
South China Sea	Arabian Sea	
Hudson Bay	Sea of Japan	

Name:_____

Going to Extremes

"EXTREME" IS MY MIDDLE NAME

The world is a grand collection of extremes. Garfield wants to see them all. This is because he has learned that the world's extremes become tourist attractions, and tourist attractions usually have refreshment stands and restaurants.

He takes a tour of these astonishing extremes:

THE WORLD'S BUSIEST SEAPORT
THE WORLD'S LONGEST UNDERSEA TUNNEL
THE WORLD'S LONGEST FJORD
THE "ROOF OF THE WORLD"
THE WORLD'S MOST DENSELY POPULATED COUNTRY
THE WORLD'S BIGGEST GLACIER

 ### The Mystery:

When Garfield takes this tour (above), will he be on continents where he can also see all of the following extremes?

- the world's largest island
- the world's longest collection of coral reefs
- the world's largest mud building

Name:_____

The Arachnid Capers

A particularly sinister group of characters carries off a series of robberies known as "The Arachnid Capers." They collect dangerous spiders and use them to frighten people. With a venomous spider held over their heads, victims are more than willing to give up treasured food, jewelry, electronics, and money.

The collection of spiders includes:

- **Brazilian wandering spiders from: 9°N, 79°W**

- **redback spiders from: 25°S, 125°E**

- **tree-dwelling funnel-web spiders from: 30°S, 132°E**

- **brown recluse spiders from: 36°N, 98°W**

- **black widow spiders from: 46°N, 121°W**

Garfield's reputation as a conqueror of spiders is known worldwide. Fortunately, police catch up with the suspects and confine them in a small cell. When Garfield arrives, he sets the spiders loose in the cell. The robbers are quick to confess and mend their evil ways. The spiders are returned to their native habitats.

🐾 The Mystery:

From what places were the spiders collected?

Name:_____

Geography Mysteries—Warm Up with Garfield

Crowded Conditions

When thousands of mice storm an area that Garfield is visiting, he's delighted to join in the capture attempts. The problem is—this place is so crowded with throngs of people that he can hardly move. It's no wonder things are crowded; this is one of the most densely populated areas of the world.

The Mysteries:

Which of these could be the area of the world where Garfield tries to chase the mice: Nunavut, Canada; along the Nile River; central Australia; western Europe; northern Russia; or Hong Kong?

What is the world population at this moment? (Visit the world population clock on the Internet at *www.census.gov/main/www/popclock.html*.)

Check the pop clock in half an hour. What is the world population now?

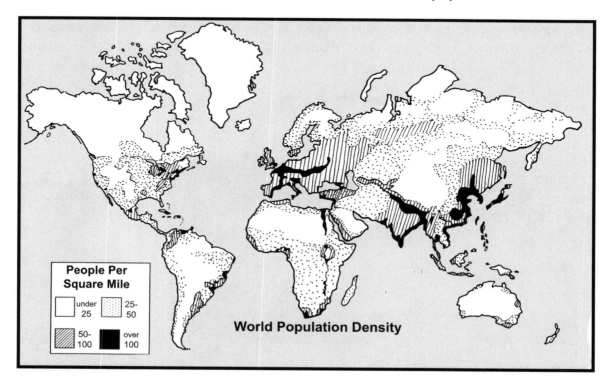

People Per Square Mile

under 25   25-50

50-100   over 100

World Population Density

Name:_____

Captured in the Canal

AH, THE LINGERING AROMAS OF RICOTTA, MOZZARELLA, AND PARMESAN CHEESE

The narrow waters of a canal provide a convenient place to trap a ship. One group of crafty characters managed to trap three freighters in one week—all in different canals. Each time, they made off with hundreds of pounds of frozen lasagna.

Garfield came along to check out the sites of the crimes. (He was hoping to find some forgotten tins of lasagna floating in the canals.) He snooped around in the three canals in this order: a canal joining Lake Superior with Lake Huron, a canal joining Lake Huron with Lake Erie, and a canal joining Lake Erie with the Hudson River.

Fortunately, he found clues that led the canal police to the suspects. They were captured in the narrow waters of a canal hundreds of miles away. This canal joined the Atlantic and Pacific Oceans. Unfortunately, most of the lasagna was long gone by then.

 The Mysteries:

What three canals did Garfield visit to hunt for clues (in the order of his visits)?

In what canal were the lasagna thieves captured?

Name:_____

The Disappearing Dogs

Garfield's List

Things to Do in the U.S.

1. EAT FRESHLY CAUGHT ATLANTIC LOBSTER
2. SAIL ON TWO GREAT LAKES
3. VISIT MT. RUSHMORE
4. HIKE THROUGH THE CUMBERLAND GAP
5. PADDLE ON THE GREAT DISMAL SWAMP
6. RIDE ACROSS THE DUST BOWL
7. CROSS TORNADO ALLEY
8. SEE DEATH VALLEY
9. BIKE AROUND THE GREAT BASIN
10. RAFT ON THE SNAKE RIVER
11. EXPLORE GLACIER NATIONAL PARK

Just as Garfield is making a list of things he plans to do on his trip around the U.S., he hears that a calamity has occurred in ten states. All the hot dogs have disappeared—not just some hot dogs, but ALL the hot dogs in the entire state in all ten states!

Garfield, the great fan of a good hot dog, rushes to these states to see if he can help solve the mystery of the disappearing dogs. (He wants to be around when the hot dogs are located!) These are the states:

Wisconsin

Nevada

Florida

Pennsylvania

Kansas

Oklahoma

Maine

Idaho

California

North Carolina

🐾 The Mystery:

Which things on his list will Garfield be able to do in the states with the missing hot dogs?

86

Copycat Crimes

Garfield finds his curiosity piqued by the case of the copycat crimes. It seems that wherever a crime was committed, within a week some copycat repeated that same crime at the exact opposite location on the globe. (For instance, a crime at **14°N, 17°W** was repeated at **14°S, 17°E.**)

 HERE ARE THE CURIOUS CRIMES:

Holes were drilled into a huge vat of enchilada sauce, emptying the vat in Encinitas, CA, USA, at **33°N, 117°W.**

All the parrots were released from their cages in São Luís, Brazil, at **25°S, 44°W.**

The garbage cans outside every building were suddenly filled with greasy chicken wings in the Maldives at **0°, 73°E.**

All the snowmobiles on the central east coast of Greenland disappeared at **74°N, 25°W.**

An upside-down screeching cat image appeared on all the computer screens in Punta Arenas, Chile, at **53°S, 70°W.**

Dozens of boats in the area of Hawaii around **19°N, 155°W** were overturned.

The Mystery: What copycat crime took place in each of these locations?

A. Coral Sea

B. Southern Colombia

C. Southwestern Australia

D. Antarctica

E. Southern Somalia

F. Kazakhstan

Name:_____

Confusion in the Mess Hall

Garfield was invited to greet the troops at seven overseas U.S. military bases. He arrived at each of these countries by boat: Crete, England, Ecuador, Japan, Spain, Guam, and Germany.

When he arrived at the first base, Garfield was told that a battalion of soldiers at each base was being deployed to Turkey. Garfield always has food on his mind, so he didn't hear the information quite right.

He thought he had been asked to "destroy the turkey." He assumed that the turkey must be hazardous to the health of the troops.

Garfield took his mission seriously and found all the turkey in the kitchen of every mess hall. He personally carried all turkey dinners, sandwiches, soup, and sausages to the garbage, causing much confusion in each mess hall.

 The Mystery:

At each stop, Garfield's boat docked on the edge of a particular body of water. Which of these would NOT be on the list of places where he docked?

- **Pacific Ocean**
- **Baltic Sea**
- **Black Sea**
- **Bay of Biscay**
- **Gulf of Aden**
- **Libyan Sea**
- **Caribbean Sea**
- **Irish Sea**
- **Sea of Japan**

UH-OH, THEY'RE LOOKING FOR THE TURKEY WHO MESSED WITH THE TURKEY

Name:_____

Pranks on the Premises

A rash of troublesome pranks is plaguing Lord Puddleton's Estate. (Purely by coincidence, this happens while Garfield is a guest there.) In a period of just three days, the host finds:

- whipped cream on windows of the room just north of the center stable.
- hundreds of spiders stuck in molasses on the structure farthest south of the vegetable garden.
- spaghetti hanging from chandeliers in the first room southwest of the kitchen.
- a greased floor in the second room east of the terrace.
- gallons of jello in all the sinks in the first room directly east of the caretaker's apartment.
- the feature just east of the Japanese garden filled with a thousand ping-pong balls.

THIS LOOKS LIKE A JOB FOR GARFIELD, THE SUPER-SLEUTH

The Mysteries:

Where . . .

1. is the jello?

2. are the spiders?

3. is the spaghetti?

4. is the greased floor?

5. are the ping-pong balls?

6. is the whipped cream?

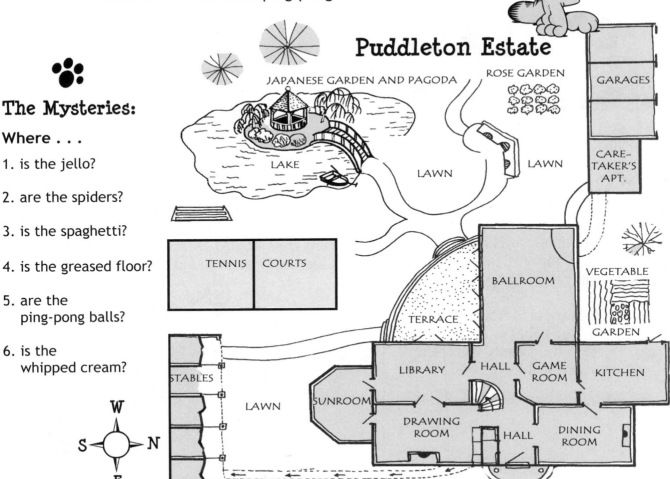

Puddleton Estate

Name:_____

Geography Mysteries—Warm Up with Garfield

The Snatched Sandwich

Nothing is quite as important to Garfield as food. When he travels, he often brings his own—just in case the food supply should be poor in the new location.

On his trip to the Canary Islands, he carries a special sandwich that he hopes will last for a few days. Imagine his distress when, as soon as he steps off the plane, the sandwich is snatched from his paws and disappears from his sight!

Slabs of salami, chunks of tuna, globs of pimento cheese, and other clues are found in several locations. They are:

- **the Dardanelles**
  - **the Galápagos Islands**
    - **Malta**
      - **the Windward Islands**
        - **Sri Lanka**

🐾 The Mysteries:

1. If Garfield starts with the location that is closest to the Canary Islands, where will he go first?

2. If Garfield starts with the location that is farthest from the Canary Islands, where will he go first?

As reports come in, Garfield consults his world map and ponders which clues to follow. He decides that he must track down all the leads. This means traveling to each of the five places where clues have been found.

The World

Name:_____

90

A Spontaneous Trip

Give Garfield the benefit of the doubt here, and suppose that the goldfish did go on a trip. Assume that the goldfish left without warning because she got an opportunity to swim in one of the world's great bays.

Keep assuming that the goldfish gets her wish and right now is happily splashing and leaping around in waters that are north of the equator, are surrounded by one country, and are connected by a strait to the Atlantic Ocean.

 The Mystery:

Which bay could this be?

- Bay of Bengal
- Hudson Bay
- Maunalua Bay
- Shark Bay
- Lamon Bay
- Bay of Biscay

Name:_____

The Last Question

It's down to the last question in the final round of the geography bee. Garfield is still in the competition! In fact, in the finals, the other contestant has just missed a question. If Garfield gets this one right, it will be the last question—and he will win!

The question:

Eight of these questions have a "no" answer. Which ones are they?

1. IS THE DEAD SEA REALLY COMPLETELY DEAD?
2. IS EASTER ISLAND A CENTER FOR RAISING EASTER BUNNIES?
3. ARE THERE REALLY DEVILS IN TASMANIA?
4. COULD YOU RIDE A TRAIN ACROSS LAKE PONTCHARTRAIN?
5. HAS NIAGARA FALLS EVER STOPPED FLOWING?
6. ARE THERE TOMBSTONES IN THE "GRAVEYARD OF THE ATLANTIC"?
7. ARE YOU LIKELY TO FIND FEMALES IN MALE?
8. IS CAPE HATTERAS SHAPED LIKE A HAT?
9. IS IT EVER CHILLY IN CHILE?
10. CAN YOU SWIM IN EL MIRAGE DRY LAKE?
11. IS A WOMBAT DESIGNED TO USE FOR HITTING BASEBALLS?
12. DOES SOMEONE OWN THE NORTH POLE?

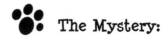 **The Mystery:**

How should Garfield answer this question in order to win the geography bee?

Name:_____

Geography Skills, Concepts, and Processes Sharpened by the Mysteries

Skill, Concept, or Process	Mystery Number(s)
Earth's revolution, rotation, tilt, hemispheres, continents, major lines of latitude and longitude	19, 21, 38, 41, 42, 52, 56, 60, 67, 71, 72, 78, 83, 87
World regions	1, 4, 7, 8, 9, 10, 12, 18, 19, 22, 23, 28, 30, 34, 36, 38, 41, 44, 46, 47, 48, 53, 54, 55, 62, 65, 66, 69, 80
World nations	1, 6, 7, 8, 9, 11, 12, 13, 20, 23, 25, 26, 27, 30, 34, 35, 39, 44, 47, 53, 54, 55, 56, 57, 58, 60, 61, 62, 63, 69, 74, 75, 76, 79, 83, 84
World cities, capital cities	1, 2, 5, 9, 23, 39, 46, 53, 54, 57, 60, 75, 83
USA and Canada, states, provinces, cities, natural features	5, 8, 14, 18, 20, 26, 32, 51, 66, 72, 73, 82
Geographic terms and features	5, 9, 11, 16, 17, 20, 25, 26, 30, 31, 32, 33, 36, 38, 42, 50, 52, 54, 55, 58, 62, 64, 65, 66, 71, 72, 76, 77, 78, 61, 84, 86, 87
Landforms	11, 13, 20, 22, 25, 26, 30, 31, 32, 33, 36, 38, 42, 49, 50, 52, 54, 55, 58, 62, 64, 65, 66, 77, 78, 86
Bodies of water	5, 9, 17, 20, 26, 28, 31, 33, 36, 42, 44, 49, 52, 54, 55, 63, 66, 69, 71, 72, 77, 78, 81, 84, 86, 87
Climate, biomes, weather	11, 28, 38, 49
Wildlife, vegetation	11, 27, 28, 60, 63, 65, 70, 79
Earth processes	30, 63
Latitude and longitude locations	1, 2, 5, 29, 38, 56, 61, 71, 72, 75, 79, 83, 87
Time zones	6, 39, 43, 51, 74, 79
Historical features	4, 14, 29, 32, 35, 41, 76
Cultural and economic features, developments, and attractions	3, 4, 10, 12, 14, 19, 25, 32, 35, 41, 46, 63, 64, 67, 68, 76, 78, 80, 82, 88
Research to find information (resources other than maps)	4, 7, 8, 10, 11, 13, 20, 22, 27, 28, 29, 30, 33, 46, 49, 57, 60, 65, 68, 72, 79, 82, 88
Use maps to locate places	1, 2, 3, 5, 6, 7, 8, 9, 13, 14, 17, 18, 19, 20, 22, 23, 24, 25, 29, 30, 31, 32, 33, 34, 35, 38, 41, 44, 47, 48, 51, 52, 53, 54, 55, 56, 57, 58, 59, 61, 62, 64, 65, 66, 68, 69, 70, 71, 72, 74, 76, 77, 79, 80, 61, 82, 83, 84, 85, 86, 87
Use maps to compare locations	1, 3, 5, 6, 8, 9, 13, 14, 17, 18, 20, 22, 23, 24, 29, 30, 31, 34, 35, 38, 41, 44, 47, 48, 51, 52, 53, 54, 55, 56, 57, 58, 59, 61, 62, 64, 65, 66, 68, 69, 70, 71, 72, 74, 76, 77, 83, 84, 86
Find directions and distances on maps	1, 3, 6, 8, 9, 14, 15, 18, 20, 23, 24, 44, 51, 53, 54, 56, 57, 58, 62, 69, 70, 85, 86
Use map features: (title, compass, key, labels, scale)	3, 14, 15, 24, 47, 56, 59, 66, 70, 85
Use a variety of maps to find information: (elevation, grid, floor plan, road, natural features, time zone, political, etc.)	all mysteries
Analyze and compare information, draw conclusions, make inferences and predictions	all mysteries

I'VE LOVED EATING MY WAY AROUND THE WORLD!

Geography Mysteries—Warm Up with Garfield

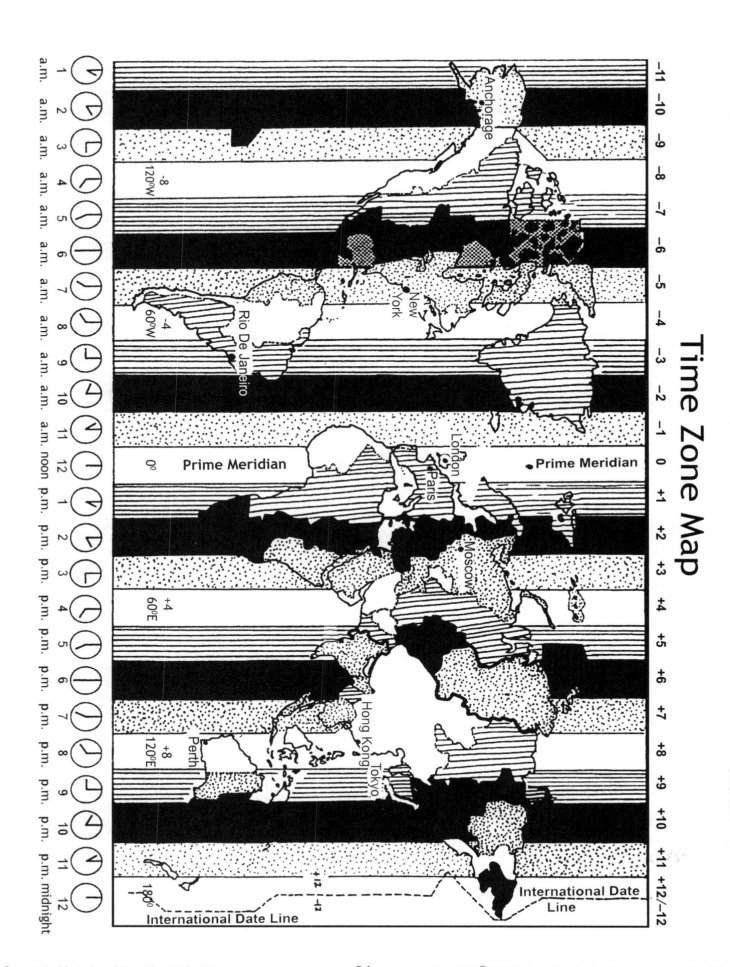

Time Zone Map

Answer Key

#1 (p 5) Port Moresby (Papua New Guinea)

#2 (p 6) May 1: Buenos Aires, Argentina; May 5: Sydney, Australia; May 8: Jakarta, Indonesia; May 14: Kingston, Jamaica; May 18: Kinshasa, Democratic Republic of the Congo (or Brazzaville, capital of the Republic of the Congo); May 22: Naples, Italy

#3 (p 7) Paintings are picked up at: 5—Palais Royale; 1—Sacre-Coeur; 7—Notre Dame; 9—Pantheon; 2—l'Arc de Triomphe; and Parc André Citroën. The original was found at Sacré-Coeur.

#4 (p 8) could be either the scrap of a priceless Persian tapestry OR the bronze statue of a Mesopotamian goddess

#5 (p 9) Adriatic Sea

#6 (p 10) Garfield reached the victim at 8:00 AM on Thursday, with four hours to spare.

#7 (p 11) 10 (in addition to Guatemala): Honduras, Saint Lucia, Mexico, Venezuela, Brazil, Nicaragua, El Salvador, Haiti, Chile, Jamaica

#8 (p 12) yes (The Confederation Bridge links Prince Edward Island with New Brunswick.) Other mysteries: Answers will vary.

#9 (p 13) the White Nile River

#10 (p 14) 1, 2, 5, 7, 8, 10; Check to see that drawings are of one of these.

#11 (p 15) There are no jungles in 5, 6, 16, 19.

#12 (p 16) Buyers from Bulgaria, Sweden, Hungary, Lithuania, and the United Kingdom do not have euros as their home currency. Other mysteries: These answers depend on the currency exchange rate between the euro and dollar and the euro and pound on the given day that students solve the mystery.

#13 (p 17) Marshall Islands

#14 (p 18) Anasazi Cliff Dwellings, Death Valley, Everglades National Park, Carlsbad Caverns, Alamo, Old Faithful

#15 (p 19) 16,000 ft

#16 (p 20) What is the point in Earth's orbit where it is farthest from the sun?

#17 (p 21) Strait of Malacca

#18 (p 22) 5; yes

#19 (p 23) Accademia Gallery in Florence, Italy, under the toe of the sculpture called "David"

#20 (p 24) b, e, f, g, i, j, n

#21 (p 25) circle 4; North America, Europe

#22 (p 26) the food supply (Cotopaxi—Ecuador)

#23 (p 27) Ukraine (city of Odessa)

#24 (p 28) the skier just above the intersection of Loony Loop and Treacherous Trail

#25 (p 29) Blue Caves of Volimes (Greece)

#26 (p 30) Province of Nunavut

#27 (p 31) Rainforest areas of northern South America

#28 (p 32) roving grizzly bears; year-round rainfall

#29 (p 33) Bezdany Raid

#30 (p 34) Mt. Etna, Italy, and Mt. Askja, Iceland, are not in the Ring of Fire area.

#31 (p 35) Tasman Sea

#32 (p 36) 1. circle C, Idaho; 2. circle E, Maryland; 3. circle A, Missouri; 4. circle B, Tennessee; 5. circle D, Kansas

#33 (p 37) Tierra del Fuego—off the southern tip of South America; Bahamas—in the Atlantic Ocean southeast of Florida and north of Cuba; Aegean Islands—Aegean Sea off the tip of Greece; Solomon Islands—south Pacific Ocean east of Papua New Guinea; Aleutians—west of Alaska stretching toward Russia in the north Pacific Ocean. There may be shallow waters or atolls that cause ships to run aground.

#34 (p 38) 15 (all but Belgium, Croatia, Lithuania, Slovakia, and Turkmenistan)

#35 (p 39) Persepolis (in Iran)

#36 (p 40) Latvia

#37 (p 41) Antarctica

#38 (p 42) Indonesia, Maldives, Gabon, Somalia, Kiribati, Kenya, Colombia, Ecuador, and Uganda

#39 (p 43) The last call came from Hawaii. Garfield receives it at 7:15 PM Monday, Hawaii time (12:15 AM Tuesday, Garfield's home time).

#40 (p 44) Circle these: the elliptical barge at the lower right corner of Khufu's tomb near the tombs of the queens; the farthest left tomb near the label "tombs of the nobles" below and left of The Great Sphinx; the tomb of the queen near the bottom of the map farthest to the right; the farthest left tomb beneath the label "tombs of the royal children"; and the Valley Temple that is just below the Great Sphinx.

#41 (p 45) Missing: ET (Eiffel Tower) and TM (Taj Mahal) notes. ET belongs where LT is now. TM belongs where P-S is now. Two are still correctly placed: P (Parthenon) and S (Stonehenge).

#42 (p 46) strait, fjord, oasis, gulf

#43 (p 47) At the time of the robbery, it was the middle of the night in Australia, not morning (12:30 AM–1:30 AM). Also, it is NOT summer in July in Australia. School would not be out, and the family would not be going to the beach.

#44 (p 48) Cambodia

#45 (p 49) 3: None were delivered to Africa, Northern Asia, or Oceania.

#46 (p 50) Items on Ireland list that belong on Scotland list: 4, 7, 8; Items on Scotland list that belong on Ireland list: 1, 5, 7

#47 (p 51) Pakistan and Oman

#48 (p 52) Yes, Garfield is correct.

#49 (p 53) 1. Antarctica; 2. Libya; 3. Kentucky, USA; 4. Austria; 5. Hawaii, USA; 6. Chile; 7. Greenland; 8. Antarctica

#50 (p 54) the stack

#51 (p 55) Theft discovered at 9 AM on Wednesday. Thief arrived in Arizona at midnight on Wednesday.

#52 (p 56) 3, 5, 8, 19

#53 (p 57) Lagunita Country Club in Caracas, Venezuela

#54 (p 58) 1. Kaliningrad, Russia; 2. Pula, Croatia; 3. Land's End, England; 4. Komárom, Hungary and Slovakia

#55 (p 59) Vanuatu, Barbados, Elba, Channel Islands

#56 (p 60) Arctic Circle—2; Antarctic Circle—0; Tropic of Cancer—3; Tropic of Capricorn—2; Equator—4; Prime Meridian—3; International Date Line—2; NOTE: Pay attention to the directions at the end of each story. In some cases, it is NOT the logical direction to follow.

#57 (p 61) Buenos Aires, Argentina (33°S latitude). Wellington, New Zealand, is the farthest south capital at 41°S latitude.

#58 (p 62) Sierra Madre Orientals, Atlas Mountains, and the Ural Mountains

#59 (p 63) Check grids to see that correct fish are colored: the farthest left fish in the fifth row, the farthest left fish entirely in the third row, the farthest right fish in the sixth row, and the farthest right fish in between the second and third rows.

#60 (p 64) Aruba; New Zealand; Murmansk, Russia; Egypt; Ho Chi Minh City, Vietnam; Vatican City; Bratislava, Slovakia; Belgrade, Serbia; and Vienna, Austria

#61 (p 65) Chile, Nicaragua, Palau, Angola, Canada, Turkmenistan, Malaysia

#62 (p 66) St. Lucia

#63 (p 67) Garfield knows: 1. There are no typhoons in the Caribbean. Typhoons occur only in the northwest Pacific Ocean. 2. There are no penguins in the Arctic. They are found only in Antarctica. 3. The aurora borealis cannot be seen from Costa Rica. 4. Maquiladoras factories are found only in Mexico.

#64 (p 68) Iberian, Musandam, Yucatan, Balkan, Malay, Jutland, Scandinavian, Sinai

#65 (p 69) Kalahari, Sahara, Arabian, Chihuahuan, Great Sandy (Mojave and Arctic are out of the latitude range; Atacama and Namib are cool coastal deserts; Gobi, Patagonia, Arctic, and Iranian are cold winter deserts.)

#66 (p 70) Lake Okeechobee (Florida)

#67 (p 71) Incorrect answers: U.S., China, Canadian, more, Africa, London, India

#68 (p 72) Australia and United States

#69 (p 73) yes

#70 (p 74) about 6 to 20 mi

#71 (p 75) Lake Chapala or Lake Texcoco; Lake Nios has exploded.

#72 (p 76) Connecticut River; north; Hanover, CT

#73 (p 77) 2 (Atlanta and Denver)

#74 (p 78) arrives in Tonga at 1:00 PM on Monday; arrives in Australia at 6:00 PM on Wednesday; arrives in Fiji at 3:00 PM on Thursday; arrives in Hawaii at 1:00 PM on Friday

#75 (p 79) A. Norway; B. North Pole; C. Guinea-Bissau; D. Myanmar; E. New Zealand

#76 (p 80) A. Falkland Islands (7); B. Australia (10); C. Crete (2); D. Cuba (9); E. Greece (4); F. Mexico (6), Canada (8), and USA (11); G. Korea (3); H. Italy (5)

#77 (p 81) South China Sea, Hudson Bay, Sea of Japan

#78 (p 82) No, the list includes sites in Europe, Asia, and Antarctica. The largest island is near North America, the longest coral reef is near Australia, and the largest mud buildings are in Africa.

#79 (p 83) Brazilian from Panama; redback from Australia; tree-dwelling funnel-web from Australia; brown recluse from Arkansas; black widow from Washington

#80 (p 84) along the Nile River, Western Europe, Hong Kong

#81 (p 85) Sault Ste. Marie Canal, Welland Canal, Erie Canal; the thieves were captured in the Panama Canal.

#82 (p 86) 1, 2, 4, 5, 6, 7, 8, 10 (9 is also allowed, as the Great Basin is sometimes defined as extending into Idaho.)

#83 (p 87) A. overturned boats; B. garbage cans filled with chicken wings; C. flowing enchilada sauce; D. snowmobiles disappeared; E. parrots released; F. cat image on computer

#84 (p 88) Black Sea, Gulf of Aden, Caribbean Sea

#85 (p 89) 1. jello—kitchen; 2. spiders—tennis court; 3. spaghetti—ballroom; 4. greased floor—drawing room; 5. ping-pong balls—lake; 6. whipped cream—sunroom

#86 (p 90) 1. Malta; 2. Sri Lanka

#87 (p 91) Hudson Bay

#88 (p 92) 1, 2, 4, 6, 8, 10, 11, 12